Charles Eliot Norton, James Russell Lowell, John Donne, Club Grolier

The Poems of John Donne

Charles Eliot Norton, James Russell Lowell, John Donne, Club Grolier

The Poems of John Donne

ISBN/EAN: 9783337168063

Printed in Europe, USA, Canada, Australia, Japan

Cover: Foto ©Thomas Meinert / pixelio.de

More available books at **www.hansebooks.com**

THE
POEMS OF JOHN DONNE

FROM THE TEXT OF THE EDITION OF 1633

REVISED BY

JAMES RUSSELL LOWELL

WITH THE VARIOUS READINGS
OF THE OTHER EDITIONS OF THE SEVENTEENTH CENTURY, AND
WITH A PREFACE, AN INTRODUCTION, AND NOTES BY

CHARLES ELIOT NORTON

———

VOLUME II

NEW-YORK
THE GROLIER CLUB
1895

CONTENTS OF VOLUME II.

LETTERS TO SEVERAL PERSONAGES.

FUNERAL ELEGIES.

DIVINE POEMS.

ELEGIES UPON THE AUTHOR.

X CONTENTS.

Note.

In the foot-notes to the present edition, the various readings are given with the dates of the editions in which they appear, except that when all the editions subsequent to that of 1633 agree in a variant, the dates are omitted.

LETTERS TO SEVERAL PERSONAGES.

LETTERS TO SEVERAL PERSONAGES.

TO MR. CHRISTOPHER BROOKE.[1]

I.

THE STORM.

Thou, which art I ('t is nothing to be so),
Thou, which art still thyself, by these[2] shalt know
Part of our passage; and a hand, or eye,
By Hilliard drawn, is worth an[3] history
By a worse painter made; and (without pride)
When by thy judgment they are dignified,
My lines are such : 't is the preëminence
Of friendship only to impute excellence.

England, to whom we owe what we be and have,
Sad that her sons did seek a foreign grave
(For Fate's or Fortune's drifts none can soothsay,[4]
Honour and misery have one face and way[5]),
From out her pregnant entrails sighed a wind,
Which at th' air's middle marble room did find
Such strong resistance that itself it threw
Downward again, and so when it did view

---

1 " From the Island Voyage with the Earl of Essex," is added in
the edition of 1635, and later editions. 2 this. 3 a. 4 gainsay,
1669. 5 one way, 1635, '39, '49, '54.

3

How in the port our fleet dear time did leese,
Withering like prisoners which lie but for fees,—
Mildly it kissed our sails, and fresh and sweet,
As to a stomach starved, whose insides meet,
Meat comes, it came and swole our sails, when we
So joyed as Sara her swelling joyed to see :
But 't was but so kind as our countrymen
Which bring friends one day's way, and leave them then;
Then, like two mighty kings which, dwelling far
Asunder, meet against a third to war,
The south and west winds joined, and, as they blew,
Waves like a rolling trench before them threw.
Sooner than you read this line, did the gale,
Like shot not feared till felt, our sails assail,
And what at first was called a gust, the same
Hath now a storm's, anon a tempest's name.
Jonas, I pity thee and curse those men
Who, when the storm raged most, did wake thee then :
Sleep is pain's easiest salve and doth fulfil
All offices of death except to kill.
But when I waked, I saw that I saw not.
I and the sun, which should teach me, had forgot
East, West, day, night ; and I could only say,
If the world had lasted, now[1] it had been day.
Thousands our noises were, yet we 'mongst all
Could none by his[2] right name, but thunder, call :
Lightning was all our light, and it rained more
Than if the sun had drunk the sea before.

1 yet, 1635, '39, '49, '54. 2 this, 1669.

Some coffined in their cabins lie, equally
Grieved that they are not dead and yet must die :
And as sin-burdened souls from grave [1] will creep
At the last day, some forth their cabins peep
And tremblingly [2] ask what news, and do hear so
Like [3] jealous husbands what they would not know ;
Some, sitting on the hatches, would seem there
With hideous gazing to fear away Fear;
Then [4] note they the ship's sicknesses, the mast
Shaked with this [5] ague, and the hold and wast
With a salt dropsy clogged ; and all our tacklings
Snapping like too high-stretchëd [6] treble-strings ;
And from our tottered [7] sails rags drop down so
As from one hanged in chains a year ago ;
Even [8] our ordnance, placed for our defence,
Strive [9] to break loose and scape away from thence.
Pumping hath tired our men, and what 's the gain?
Seas into seas thrown we suck in again :
Hearing hath deafed our sailors, and if they
Knew how to hear, there 's none knows what to say.
Compared to these storms, death is but a qualm,
Hell somewhat lightsome, and the Bermuda calm : [10]
Darkness, light's eldest brother, his birthright
Claimed o'er this [11] world, and to heaven hath chased light :
All things are one, and that one none can be,
Since all forms uniform deformity

---

1 graves, 1669. 2 trembling. 3 As. 4 There, 1669. 5 an. 6 like too too high-
    stretched, 1635, '39, '49, '54 ; like to too high-stretched, 1669. 7 tattered.
    8 Yea, ev'n. 9 Strives. 10 lightsome, the Bermudas calm. 11 Claims
    o'er the.
II.— 1*

Doth cover, so that we, except God say
Another *Fiat*, shall have no more day.
So violent, yet long, these furies be,
That though thine absence starve me, I wish not thee.

II.

THE CALM.

OUR storm is past, and that storm's tyrannous rage
A stupid calm, but nothing it, doth suage.
The fable is inverted, and far more
A block afflicts now than a stork before.
Storms chafe, and soon wear out themselves or us;
In calms Heaven laughs to see us languish thus.
As steady as I can wish that my thoughts were,[1]
Smooth as thy mistress' glass or what shines there,
The sea is now, and as the isles which we
Seek, when we can move, our ships rooted be.
As water did in storms, now pitch runs out
As lead when a fired church becomes one spout,
And all our beauty and our trim decays,
Like courts removing or like ended[2] plays.
The fighting-place now seamen's rags[3] supply,
And all the tackling is a frippery.
No[4] use of lanterns; and in one place lay
Feathers and dust, to-day and yesterday.

1 could wish my thoughts were. 2 ending, 1669. 3 rage, *ibid.*
4 Now, *ibid.*

Earth's hollownesses, which the world's lungs are,
Have no more wind than the upper vault of air ;
We can nor lost friends nor sought foes recover,
But meteor-like, save that we move not, hover.
Only the calenture together draws
Dear friends, which meet dead in great fishes' jaws ; [1]
And on the hatches, as on altars, lies
Each one, his own priest, and own sacrifice.
Who live, that miracle do multiply
Where walkers in hot ovens do not die :
If in despite of these we swim, that hath
No more refreshing than our [2] brimstone-bath,
But from the sea into the ship we turn
Like parboiled wretches on the coals to burn.
Like Bajazet encaged, the shepherds' scoff,
Or like slack-sinewed Samson, his hair off,
Languish our ships. Now as a myriad
Of ants durst th' emperor's loved snake invade,
The crawling gallies, sea-goales,[3] finny chips,
Might brave our venices, now bed-rid ships.[4]
Whether a rotten state and hope of gain,
Or to disuse me from the queasy pain
Of being beloved and loving, or the thirst
Of honour or fair death outpushed me first,
I lose my end ; for here as well as I
A desperate may live and a coward [5] die.
Stag, dog, and all which from or towards flies,
Is paid with life or prey, or doing dies ;

1 maws. 2 a. 3 sea-gulls. 4 pinnaces, now bed-rid ships, 1635, '39,
'49, '54 ; with Vinices our bed-rid ships, 1669. 5 and coward.

Fate grudges us all, and doth subtly lay
A scourge 'gainst which we all forget [1] to pray.
He that at sea prays for more wind, as well
Under the poles may beg cold, heat in hell.
What are we then?   How little more, alas,
Is man now than before he was he was!
Nothing for us, we are for nothing fit;
Chance or ourselves still disproportion it;
We have no power, no will, no sense; I lie,
I should not then thus feel this misery.

TO SIR HENRY WOTTON.

Sir, more than kisses, letters mingle souls,
For thus friends absent speak.   This ease controls
The tediousness of my life: but for these
I could ideate nothing which could please,[2]
But I should wither in one day and pass
To a bottle of hay, that am a lock of grass.[3]
Life is a voyage, and in our life's ways
Countries, courts, towns are rocks or remoras;
They break or stop all ships, yet our state 's such
That, though than pitch they stain worse, we must touch.
If in the furnace of the raging[4] Line,
Or under th' adverse icy Pole thou pine,

---

1 forgot, 1669.   2 I could invent nothing at all to please, *ibid*.   3 To
a lock of hay, that am a bottle of grass, *ibid*.   4 even, *ibid*.

Thou know'st two temperate regions girded in
Dwell there; but oh! what refuge canst thou win,
Parched in the court and in the country frozen?
Shall cities built of both extremes be chosen?
Can dung and garlic be a perfume?[1] Or can
A scorpion or torpedo cure a man?
Cities are worst of all three; of all three
(Oh knotty riddle) each is worst equally.
Cities are sepulchres; they who dwell there
Are carcasses, as if no such they were;[2]
And courts are theatres where some men play
Princes, some slaves, all to one end, and of one clay.[3]
The country is a desert, where no good
Gained as habits, not born, is understood;[4]
There men become beasts and prone to more evils;[5]
In cities, blocks; and in a lewd court, devils.
As in the first Chaos confusedly
Each element's qualities were in the other three,
So pride, lust, covetise, being several
To these three places, yet all are in all,
And mingled thus, their issue[6] incestuous:
Falsehood is denizened; Virtue is barbarous.
Let no man say there, " Virtue's flinty wall
Shall lock vice in me; I'll do none, but know all."
Men are sponges, which, to pour out, receive;
Who know false play, rather than lose, deceive.

1 dung or garlic be perfume? 1635, '39, '49, '54; dung or garlic be
a perfume? 1669. 2 none such there were. 3 all to one end,
of one clay, 1635, '39; of one day, 1649, '54; and all end in
one day, 1669. 4 the good, Gained inhabits not, born, is not
understood, 1635, '39, '49, '54. 5 all evils. 6 issue is.

For in best understandings sin began ;
Angels sinned first, then devils, and then man.
Only perchance beasts sin not ; wretched we
Are beasts in all but white integrity.
I think if men which in these places live
Durst look in themselves and themselves retrieve,
They would like strangers greet themselves, seeing than
Utopian youth, grown old, Italiän.

Be thou[1] thine own home and in thyself dwell ;
Inn anywhere ; continuance maketh hell.
And seeing the snail which everywhere doth roam,
Carrying his own house still, still is at home,
Follow (for he is easy paced) this snail ;
Be thine own palace, or the world 's thy jail.
And in the world's sea, do not like cork sleep
Upon the water's face, nor in the deep
Sink like a lead without a line, but as
Fishes glide, leaving no print where they pass
Nor making sound, so closely thy course go ;
Let men dispute whether thou breathe or no :
Only in this one thing be[2] no Galenist,— to make
Court's hot ambitions wholesome, do not take
A dram of country's dullness ; do not add
Correctives, but, as chymics, purge the bad ;
But, Sir, I advise not you, I rather do
Say o'er those lessons which I learned of you,
Whom, free from German[3] schisms, and lightness
Of France, and fair Italy's faithlessness,

1 Be then. 2 in this be. 3 Germany's.

Having from these sucked all they had of worth,
And brought home that faith which you carried forth,
I throughly love; but if myself I have won
To know my rules, I have and you have

DONNE.

TO SIR HENRY GOODYERE.

Who makes the past[1] a pattern for next year,
　Turns no new leaf, but still the same things reads,
Seen things he sees again, heard things doth hear,
　And makes his life but like a pair of beads.

A palace, when 't is that which it should be,
　Leaves growing and stands such, or else decays;
But he which dwells there is not so, for he
　Strives to urge upward and his fortune raise.

So had your body her morning, hath her noon,
　And shall not better; her next change is night:
But her fair larger guest, to whom sun and moon
　Are sparks and short-lived, claims another right.

The noble soul by age grows lustier,
　Her appetite and her digestion mend;
We must not starve, nor hope to pamper her
　With women's[2] milk and pap unto the end.

1 last, 1669.　2 woman's, *ibid.*

Provide you manlier diet; you have seen
  All libraries, which are schools, camps, and courts;
But ask your garners if you have not been
  In harvests too indulgent to your sports.

Would you redeem it?   Then yourself transplant
  Awhile from hence. Perchance outlandish ground
Bears no more wit than ours; but yet more scant
  Are those diversions there, which here abound.

To be a stranger hath that benefit,
  We can beginnings but not habits choke:
Go whither? hence; you get, if you forget;
  New faults, till they prescribe in[1] us, are smoke.

Our soul, whose country is Heaven and God her father,
  Into this world, corruption's sink, is sent;
Yet so much in her travel she doth gather,
  That she returns home wiser than she went.

It pays you well, if it teach you to spare,
  And make you ashamed to make your hawk's praise
    yours,
Which, when herself she lessens in the air,
  You then first say that high enough she towers.

However, keep the lively taste you hold
  Of God; love him as now,[2] but fear him more;
And in your afternoons think what you told
  And promised him at morning-prayer before.

1 to. 2 love him now, 1639, '49, '54, '69.

Let falsehood like a discord anger you ;
  Else be not froward : but why do I touch
Things of which none is in your practice new,
  And tables [1] or fruit-trenchers teach as much ?

But thus I make you keep your promise, Sir ;
  Riding I had you, though you still stayed there,
And in these thoughts, although you never stir,
  You came with me to Micham, and are here.

TO MR. ROWLAND WOODWARD.

LIKE one, who in her third widowhood doth profess
Herself a nun tied to retiredness,
So affects my Muse now a chaste fallowness ;

Since she to few, yet to too many, hath shown [2]
How love-song weeds, [3] and satyric thorns are grown
Where seeds of better arts were early sown.

Though to use and love poetry, to me,
Betrothed to no one art, be no adultery,
Omissions of good ill as ill deeds be.

For though to us it seem and be [4] light and thin,
Yet in those faithful scales, where God throws in
Men's works, vanity weighs as much as sin.

1 fables, 1669. 2 flown, 1635, '39, '49, '54. 3 How long love's
weeds, 1635, '39, '49, '54. 4 seem but.

If our souls have stained their first white, yet we
May clothe them with faith and dear honesty,
Which God imputes as native purity.

There is no virtue but religiön :
Wise, valiant, sober, just, are names which none
Want which want not vice-covering discretion.

Seek we then ourselves in ourselves ; for as
Men force the sun with much more force to pass
By gathering his beams with a crystal glass,

So we (if we into ourselves will turn,
Blowing our sparks [1] of virtue,) may outburn
The straw which doth about our hearts sojourn.

You know physicians, when they would infuse
Into any oil the souls of simples, use
Places where they may lie still warm to choose.

So works retiredness in us; to roam
Giddily, and be everywhere but at home,
Such freedom doth a banishment become.

We are but termers [2] of ourselves ; yet may,
If we can stock ourselves and thrive, uplay
Much, much dear [3] treasure for the great rent-day.

Manure thyself then, to thyself be approved, [4]
And with vain outward things be no more moved
But to know that I love thee and would be loved.

1 spark, 1669. 2 farmers. 3 good. 4 improved, 1669.

TO SIR HENRY WOTTON.

HERE 's no more news [1] than virtue ; I may as well
Tell you Calais' or Saint Michael's tale for news, as tell [2]
That vice doth here habitually dwell.

Yet as to get stomachs we walk up and down,
And toil to sweeten rest ; so may God frown
If, but to loathe both, I haunt Court or [3] town.

For here no one is from the extremity
Of vice by any other reason free,
But that the next to him still is worse than he.

In this world's warfare they whom rugged Fate
(God's commissary) doth so throughly hate
As in the Court's squadron to marshál their state,

If they stand armed with seely honesty,
With wishing [4] prayers, and neat integrity,
Like Indians 'gainst Spanish hosts they be.

Suspicious boldness to this place belongs,
And to have as many ears as all have tongues,
Tender to know, tough to acknowledge wrongs.

Believe me, Sir, in my youth's giddiest days,
When to be like the Court was a play's [5] praise,
Plays were not so like Courts as Courts are like [6] plays.

---

[1] new, 1669. [2] tales, as tell, 1635, '39, '49, '54. Tell Calais or St. Michael's
Mount, as tell, 1669. [3] and, *ibid.* [4] wishes, 1635, '39, '49, '54. [5] play-
er's, 1639, '49, '54, '69. [6] Courts like.

Then let us at these mimic antics jest,
Whose deepest projects and egregious gests
Are but dull morals of[1] a game at chests.

But now 't is incongruity[2] to smile,
Therefore I end, and bid farewell a while
At Court, though *from Court* were the better style.

TO THE COUNTESS OF BEDFORD.

Madam,

REASON is our soul's left hand, Faith her right;
By these we reach divinity,—that 's you :
Their loves, who have the blessings[3] of your light,
Grew from their Reason; mine from fair Faith grew.

But as, although a squint left-handedness
Be ungracious, yet we cannot want that hand,
So would I (not to increase, but to express
My faith) as I believe, so understand.

Therefore I study you first in your saints,
Those friends whom your election glorifies;
Then in your deeds, accesses, and restraints,
And what you read, and what yourself devise.

---

[1] are egregious guests, And but dull morals at, 1669. [2] But 't is an incongruity, *ibid.* [3] blessing.

But soon the reasons why you 're loved by all
Grow infinite, and so pass Reason's reach,
Then back again to implicit Faith I fall,
And rest on what the catholic faith [1] doth teach,—

That you are good : and not one heretic
Denies it ; if he did, yet you are so ;
For rocks which high-topped and deep-rooted stick,[2]
Waves wash, not undermine, nor overthrow.

In everything there naturally grows
A balsamum to keep it fresh and new,
If 't were not injured by extrinsic blows ;
Your birth and beauty are this balm in you.

But you of learning and religiön
And virtue and such ingredients have made
A mithridate whose operatiön
Keeps off or cures what can be done or said.

Yet this is not your physic, but your food,
A diet fit for you ; for you are here
The first good angel, since the world's frame stood,
That ever did in woman's shape appear.

Since you are then God's masterpiece, and so
His factor for our loves, do as you do ;
Make your return home gracious, and bestow
Thy life [3] on that ; so make one life of two :
    For so God help me, I would not miss you there
    For all the good which you can do me here.

1 voice. 2 high to sense, deep-rooted stick, 1635, '39, '49, '54 ;
high do seem, 1669. 3 This life.

TO THE COUNTESS OF BEDFORD.

MADAM,
You have refined me ; and to worthiest things,
Virtue, art, beauty, fortune ; now I see
Rareness or use, not nature, value brings,
And such as they are circumstanced they be.
    Two ills can ne'er perplex us sin to excuse,
    But of two good things we may leave and [1] choose.

Therefore at Court, which is not Virtue's clime,
Where a transcendent height (as lowness me)
Makes her not be,[2] or not show, all my rhyme
Your virtues challenge, which there rarest be ;
    For as dark texts need notes, there some [3] must be
    To usher Virtue and say *This is she.*

So in the country is beauty.   To this place
You are the season, (Madam) you the day,
'T is but a grave of spices till your face
Exhale them, and a thick, close bud display.
    Widowed and reclused else, her sweets she enshrines
    As China when the sun at Brazil dines.

Out from your chariot morning breaks at night,
And falsifies both computations so ;
Since a new world doth rise here from your light,
We your new creatures by new reckonings go :

[1] or, 1669.   [2] see, *ibid.*   [3] some there, *ibid.*

This shows that you from nature loathly stray,
That suffer not an artificial day.

In this you 've made the Court the antipodes,
And willed your delegate, the vulgar sun,
To do profane autumnal offices,
Whilst here to you we sacrificers run ;
  And whether priests or organs, you we obey,
  We sound your influence and your dictates say.

Yet to that deity which dwells in you,
Your virtuous soul, I now not sacrifice ;
These are petitions and not hymns ; they sue
But that I may survey the edifice.
  In all religions as much care hath bin
  Of temples' frames and beauty, as rites within.

As all which go to Rome, do not thereby
Esteem religions and hold fast the best,
But serve discourse and curiosity
With that which doth religion but invest,
  And shun th' entangling labyrinths of schools,
  And make it wit to think the wiser fools ;—

So in this pilgrimage I would behold
You as you 're Virtue's temple, not as she ;
What walls of tender crystal her enfold,
What eyes, hands, bosom, her pure altars be,
  And after this survey oppose to all
  Babblers [1] of chapels, you, th' Escurial.

1 Builders, 1669.

Yet not as consecrate, but merely as fair,
On these I cast a lay and country eye.
Of past and future stories which are rare,
I find you all recórd and prophecy.
    Purge but the book of Fate that it admit
    No sad nor guilty legends,—you are it.

If good and lovely were not one, of both
You were the transcript and original,
The elements, the parent,[1] and the growth,
And every piece of you is both[2] their all :
    So entire are all your deeds and you, that you
    Must do the same things still; you cannot two.

But these (as nice thin school-divinity[3]
Serves heresy to further or repress)
Taste of poetic rage or flattery,
And need not, where all hearts one truth profess;
    Oft from new proofs and new phrase new doubts grow,
    As strange attire aliens[4] the men we know.

Leaving then busy praise and all[5] appeal
To higher courts, sense's decree is true ;
The mine, the magazine, the commonweal,
The story of beauty, in Twicknam is and you ;
    Who hath seen one, would both ; as who had[6] bin
    In paradise, would seek the Cherubin.

---

[1] parents, 1669.   [2] worth.   [3] nicest school divinity, 1669.   [4] alters, 1635, '39, '49, '54.   [5] end all, 1669.   [6] hath, 1639, '49, '54, '69.

TO SIR EDWARD HERBERT, AT JULIERS.[1]

Man is a lump where all beasts kneaded be ;
Wisdom makes him an ark where all agree ;
The fool, in whom these beasts do live at jar,
Is sport to others and a theater :
Nor scapes he so, but is himself their prey ;
All which was man in him is eat away ;
And now his beasts on one another feed,
Yet couple in anger and new monsters breed.
How happy is he which hath due place assigned
To his beasts and disaforested his mind,
Empaled himself to keep them out, not in,
Can sow, and dares trust corn, where they have bin
Can use his horse, goat, wolf, and every beast,
And is not ass himself to all the rest !
Else man not only is the herd of swine,
But he 's those devils, too, which did incline
Them to a headlong[2] rage and made them worse ;
For man can add weight to heaven's heaviest curse.
As souls (they say) by our first touch take in
The poisonous tincture of original sin,
So, to the punishments which God doth fling,
Our apprehension cóntributes the sting.
To us, as to his chickens, he doth cast
Hemlock, and we, as men, his hemlock taste ;

[1] Now Lord Herbert of Cherbury, being at the siege of Juliers,
1635, '39, '49, '54. Since Lord Herbert, etc., 1669. [2] au
headlong, 1635, '39, '49, '54 ; to headlong, 1669.
II.— 2*

We do infuse to what he meant for meat
Corrosiveness, or intense cold or heat :
For God no such specific poison hath
As kills we [1] know not how; his fiercest wrath
Hath no antipathy, but may be good
At least for physic, if not for our food.
Thus man, that might be his pleasure, is his rod,
And is his devil, that might be his God.
Since then our business is to rectify
Nature to what she was, we 're led awry
By them who man to us in little show ;
Greater than due, no form we can bestow
On him; for man into himself can draw
All; all his faith can swallow or reason chaw,
All that is filled, and all that which doth fill ;
All the round world to man is but a pill ;
In all it works not, but it is in all
Poisonous or purgative or cordiäl.
For knowledge kindles calentures in some,
And is to others icy opium.
As brave as true is that profession than,
Which you do use to make,— that you know man.
This makes it credible you have dwelt upon
All worthy books, and now are such an one :
Actions are authors, and of those in you
Your friends find every day a mart of new.

---

[1] men.

TO THE COUNTESS OF BEDFORD.

T' HAVE written then, when you writ, seemed to me
Worst of spiritual vices, simony ;
And not t' have written then, seems little less
Than worst of civil vices, thanklessness.
In this, my debt[1] I seemed loath to confess,
In that, I seemed to shun beholdingness :
But 't is not so : nothing,[2] as I am, may
Pay all they have and yet have all to pay.
Such borrow in their payments and owe more
By having leave to write so than before.
Yet, since rich mines in barren grounds are shown,
May not I yield, not gold, but coal or stone ?
Temples were not demolished, though profane ;
Here Peter Jove's, there Paul have[3] Dian's fane.
So whether my hymns you admit or choose,
In me you have hallowèd a pagan muse
And denizened a stranger, who, mistaught
By blamers of the times they marred, hath sought
Virtues in corners, which now bravely do
Shine in the world's best part, or all,— in you.[4]
I have been told that virtue in courtiers' hearts
Suffers an ostracism and departs.
Profit, ease, fitness, plenty bid it go,
But whither, only knowing you, I know ;

[1] doubt, 1633. [2] nothings, 1635, '39, '49, '54. [3] hath.
[4] or all it ; you.

Your, or you virtue,[1] two vast uses serves,
It ransoms one sex and one court preserves;
There 's nothing but your worth, which, being true,
Is known to any other, not to you;
And you can never know it; to admit
No knowledge of your worth, is some of it.
But since to you your praises discords be,
Stop[2] others' ills to meditate with me.
Oh! to confess we know not what we should
Is half excuse we know not what we would.
Lightness depresseth us, emptiness fills;
We sweat and faint, yet still go down the hills;
As new philosophy arrests the sun,
And bids the passive earth about it run,
So we have dulled our mind; it hath no ends;
Only the body 's busy and pretends:
As dead low earth eclipses and controls
The quick high moon, so doth the body souls.
In none but us are such mixed engines found
As hands of double office; for the ground
We till with them, and them to heaven we raise;
Who prayerless labours, or without this[3] prays,
Doth but one half; that 's none; He which said, *Plough,
And look not back*, to *look up* doth allow.
Good seed degenerates, and oft obeys
The soil's disease and into cockle strays:
Let the[4] mind's thoughts be but transplanted so
Into the body, and bastardly they grow.

1 You, or you virtue, 1669.   2 Stoop.   3 these, 1669.
4 Let but the, *ibid.*

What hate could hurt our bodies like our love?
We, but no foreign tyrans, could remove
These, not ingraved, but inborn dignities,
Caskets of souls, temples and palaces.
For bodies shall from death redeemèd be,
Souls but preserved, not [1] naturally free;
As men to our prisons, new souls [2] to us are sent,
Which learn it [3] there and come in innocent.
First seeds of every creature are in us;
Whate'er the world hath bad or precious,
Man's body can produce: hence hath it been,
That stones, worms, frogs, and snakes in man are seen:
But who e'er saw, though nature can work so,
That pearl, or gold, or corn in man did grow?
We have added to the world Virginia, and sent
Two new stars lately to the firmament;
Why grudge we us (not Heaven) the dignity
T' increase with ours those fair souls' company?
But I must end this letter; though it do
Stand on two truths, neither is true to you.
Virtue hath some perverseness, for she will
Neither believe her good nor others' ill.
Even in your virtue's best [4] paradise
Virtue hath some, but wise, degrees of vice.
Too many virtues, or too much of one
Begets in you unjust suspicïon,
And ignorance of vice makes virtue less,
Quenching compassion of our wretchedness.

1 born. 2 now, souls. 3 vice. 4 Even in you, virtue's best.

But these are riddles; some aspersiön
Of vice becomes well some complexiön.
Statesmen purge vice with vice, and may corrode
The bad with bad, a spider with a toad;
For so ill thralls not them, but they tame ill
And make her do much good against her will;
But in your commonwealth or world, in you,
Vice hath no office or good work to do.
Take then no vicious purge, but be content
With cordial virtue, your known nourishment.

TO THE COUNTESS OF BEDFORD.

ON NEW-YEAR'S DAY.

THIS twilight of two years, not past, nor next
   Some emblem is of me, or I of this,
Who meteor-like, of stuff and form perplext,
   Whose *what* and *where* in disputation is,
   If I should call me *anything*, should miss.

I sum the years and me, and find me not
   Debtor to th' old, nor creditor to th' new:
That cannot say, my thanks I have forgot;
   Nor trust I this with hopes; and yet scarce true
   This bravery is,—since these time[1] showed me you.

[1] times.

In recompense I would show future times
 What you were, and teach them to urge towards such.
Verse embalms virtue, and tombs or thrones of rhymes
 Preserve frail transitory fame as much
 As spice doth bodies from corrupt airs' touch.

Mine are short-lived; the tincture of your name
 Creates in them, but dissipates as fast,
New spirit;[1] for strong agents with the same
 Force that doth warm and cherish us, do waste;
 Kept hot with strong extracts no bodies last.

So my verse, built of your just praise, might want
 Reason and likelihood, the firmest base,
And, made of miracle, now faith is scant,
 Will vanish soon and so possess no place;
 And you and it too much grace might disgrace.

When all (as truth commands assent) confess
 All truth of you, yet they will doubt how I,
One corn of one low ant-hill's dust, and less,
 Should name, know, or express a thing so high,
 And not an inch, measure infinity.

I cannot tell them nor myself nor you,
 But leave, lest truth be endangered by my praise,
And turn to God who knows I think this true,
 And useth oft, when such a heart missays,
 To make it good; for such a prayer[2] prays.

1 spirits. 2 praiser.

He will best teach you how you should lay out
   His stock of beauty, learning, favour, blood;
He will perplex security with doubt,
   And clear those doubts; hide from you, and show you
      good,
   And so increase your appetite and food.

He will teach you that good and bad have not
   One latitude in cloisters and in court;
Indifferent there the greatest space hath got;
   Some pity 's not good there; [1] some vain disport,
   On this side sin, with that place may comport.

Yet he, as he bounds seas, will fix your hours,
   Which pleasure and delight may not ingress;
And though what none else lost, be truliest yours,
   He will make you, what you did not, possess,
   By using others' (not vice, but) weakness.

He will make you speak truths, and credibly,
   And make you doubt that others do not so;
He will provide you keys and locks, to spy
   And scape spies to good ends; and he will show
   What you may [2] not acknowledge, what not know.

For your own conscience he gives innocence,
   But for your fame a discreet wariness,
And though to scape than to revenge offence
   Be better, he shows both, and to repress
   Joy, when your state swells, sadness, when 't is less.

1 Some piety 's not good here [in court] (?).— J. R. L.   2 will, 1669.

From need of tears he will defend your soul,
  Or make a rebaptizing of one tear ;
He cannot (that 's, he will not) disenroll
  Your name ; and when with active joy we hear
This private gospel, then 't is our new year.

TO THE COUNTESS OF HUNTINGDON.

MADAM,
MAN to God's image, Eve to man's [1] was made,
  Nor find we that God breathed a soul in her;
Canons will not church-functions you invade,
  Nor laws to civil office you prefer.

Who vagrant transitory comets sees,
  Wonders because they 're rare ; but a new star
Whose motion with the firmament agrees,
  Is miracle ; for there no new things are.

In woman [2] so perchance mild innocence
  A seldom comet is ; but active good
A miracle which reason scapes and sense ;
  For Art and Nature this in them withstood.

As such a star which Magi [3] led to view
  The manger-cradled infant, God below,
By virtue's beams (by fame derived from you)
  May apt souls, and the worst may, virtue know.

1 to man, 1649, '54, '69. 2 women, 1669. 3 the Magi.

If the world's age and death be argued well
   By the sun's fall which now towards earth doth bend,
Then we might fear that virtue, since she fell
   So low as woman, should be near her end.

But she 's not stooped, but raised; exiled by men,
   She fled to Heaven, that 's heavenly things, that 's you;
She was in all men thinly scattered then
   But now, amassed,[1] contracted in a few.

She gilded us; but you are gold and she;
   Us she informed,[2] but transubstantiates you :
Soft dispositiöns which ductile be,
   Elixir-like, she makes not clean, but new.

Though you a wife's and mother's name retain,
   'T is not as woman, for all are not so;
But Virtue, having made you virtue, is fain
   T' adhere in these names, her and you to show.

Else, being alike pure, we should neither see;
   As water, being into air rarefied,
Neither appear, till in one cloud they be,
   So for our sakes you do low names abide.

Taught by great constellations, (which, being framed
   Of the most stars, take low names, Crab and Bull,
When single planets by the gods are named)
   You covet not great names, of great things full.

1 a mass.   2 Informéd us.

So you, as woman, one doth comprehend,
    And in the veil of kindred others see ;
To some you are revealed as in a friend,
    And as a virtuous prince far off, to me.

To whom, because from you all virtues flow,
    And 't is not none to dare contemplate you,
I which to you[1] as your true subject owe
    Some tribute for that, so these lines are due.

If you can think these flatteries, they are ;
    For then your judgment is below my praise ;
If they were so, oft flatteries work as far
    As counsels, and as far th' endeavour raise.

So my ill, reaching you, might there grow good,
    But I remain a poisoned fountain still ;
But not your beauty, virtue, knowledge, blood,
    Are more above all flattery than my will.

And if I flatter any, 't is not you,
    But my own judgment, who did long ago
Pronounce that all these praises should be true,
    And virtue should your beauty and birth outgrow.

Now that my prophecies are all fulfilled,
    Rather than God should not be honoured too
And all these gifts confessed which he instilled,
    Yourself were bound to say that which I do.

1 do so.

So I but your recorder am in this,
     Or mouth, or [1] speaker of the universe,
A ministerial notary ; for 't is
     Not I, but you and Fame, that make this verse ;

I was your prophet in your younger days,
And now your chaplain, God in you to praise.

TO MR. I. W.

ALL hail, sweet Poet, more full [2] of more strong fire
     Than hath or shall enkindle any spirit ! [3]
     I loved what nature gave thee ; but this [4] merit
Of wit and art I love not, but admire ;
Who have before or shall write after thee,
Their works, though toughly laboured, will be
     Like infancy or age to man's firm stay,
     Or early and late twilights to mid-day.

Men say, and truly, that they better be
     Which be envíed than pitied ; therefore I,
     Because I wish thee best, do thee envý :
Oh wouldst thou by like reason pity me !
But care not for me,—I, that ever was
In Nature's and in Fortune's gifts, alas,
     (Before [by] thy [5] grace got in the Muses' school)
     A monster and a beggar, am a fool !

[1] and.   [2] and full, 1669.   [3] my dull spirit.   [4] thy.   [5] But for thy.

Oh how I grieve that late-born modesty
   Hath got such root in easy waxen hearts
   That men may not themselves their own good parts
Extol without suspect of surquedry ;
For, but thyself, no subject can be found
Worthy thy quill, nor any quill resound
   Thy work [1] but thine : how good it were to see
   A poem in thy praise, and writ by thee !

Now if this song be too harsh for rhyme, yet as
   The painter's bad god made a good [2] devil,
   'T will be good prose, although the verse be evil,
If thou forget the rhyme as thou dost pass ;
Then write, then [3] I may follow, and so be
Thy debtor, thy echo, [4] thy foil, thy zany.
   I shall be thought, if mine like thine I shape,
   All the world's lion, though I be thy ape.

TO MR. T. W.

Haste thee, harsh verse, as fast as thy lame measure
Will give thee leave, to him.   My pain and pleasure,
I have given thee, and yet thou art too weak,
Feet, and a reasoning soul, and tongue to speak.
Tell him all questions which men have defended
Both of the place and pains of hell are ended ;

---

[1] worth, 1669.   [2] goodly (?).— J. R. L.   [3] that, 1669.
[4] Thy echo, thy debtor, *ibid.*

II.—3

And 't is decreed our hell is but privation
Of him, at least in this earth's habitation :
And 't is where I am, where in every street
Infections follow, overtake, and meet.
Live I or die, by you my love is sent ;
And you 're [1] my pawns, or else my testament.

TO MR. T. W.

Pregnant again with th' old twins, Hope and Fear,
Oft have I asked for thee, both how and where
Thou wert, and what my hopes of letters were ;

As in our streets sly beggars narrowly
Watch motions of the giver's hand or eye,
And evermore conceive some hope thereby.

And now thy alms is given, thy letter 's read,
The body risen again the which was dead,
And thy poor starveling bountifully fed.

After this banquet my soul doth say grace
And praise thee for 't, and zealously embrace
Thy love ; though I think thy [2] love in this case
    To be as gluttons', which say midst their meat,
    They love that best of which they most do eat.

1 You are.   2 my (?).— J. R. L.

INCERTO.[1]

AT once from hence my lines and I depart,
I to my soft, still walks, they to my[2] heart;
I to the nurse, they to the child of art.

Yet as a firm house, though the carpenter
Perish, doth stand; as an ambassador
Lies safe, howe'er his king be in dangér,

So, though I languish, pressed with melancholy,
My verse, the strict map of my misery,
Shall live to see that for whose want I die.

Therefore I envy them and do repent
That from unhappy me things happy are sent;
Yet as a picture or bare sacrament
  Accept these lines, and if in them there be
  Merit of love, bestow that love on me.

TO MR. C. B.

THY friend, whom thy deserts to thee enchain,
  Urged by this unexcusable occasion,
  Thee and the saint of his affection
Leaving behind, doth of both wants complain;

1 Without title in 1633. 2 thy (?).— J. R. L.

And let the love I bear to both sustain
   No blot nor maim by this division;
   Strong is this love which ties our hearts in one,
And strong that love pursued with amorous pain :
But though besides thyself[1] I leave behind
   Heaven's liberal and earth's thrice-fair[2] sun,
   Going to where stern[3] winter aye doth won;
Yet love's hot fires which martyr my sad mind
   Do send forth scalding sighs which have the art
   To melt all ice but that which walls her heart.

TO MR. S. B.

O THOU, which to search out the secret parts
   Of the India, or rather paradise,
   Of knowledge, hast with courage and advice
Lately launched into the vast sea of arts,
Disdain not in thy constant travelling
   To do as other voyagers, and make
   Some turns into less creeks, and wisely take
Fresh water at the Heliconian spring.
I sing not, Siren-like, to tempt; for I
   Am harsh, nor as those schismatics with you,
   Which draw all wits of good hope to their crew;
But seeing in you bright sparks of poetry,
   I, though I brought no fuel, had desire
   With these articulate blasts to blow the fire.

1 myself, 1669.
2 and the thrice-fair, 1635, '39, '49, '54; fairer (?).—J. R. L. 3 sterved.

TO MR. B. B.

Is not thy sacred hunger of sciénce
    Yet satisfied? is not thy brain's rich hive
Fulfilled with honey which thou dost derive
From the arts' spirits and their quíntessence?
Then wean thyself at last, and thee withdraw
    From Cambridge, thy old nurse; and, as the rest,
    Here toughly chew and sturdily digest
Th' immense vast volumes of our common law;
And begin soon, lest my grief grieve thee too,
    Which is that that which I should have begun
    In my youth's morning, now late must be done,
And I as giddy travellers must do,
    Which stray or sleep all day, and, having lost
    Light and strength, dark and tired must then ride post.

If thou unto thy Muse be marriëd,
    Embrace her ever, ever multiply;
    Be far from me that strange adultery
To tempt thee and procure her widowhood;[1]
My Muse[2] (for I had one) because I 'm cold,
    Divorced herself, the cause being in me;
    That I can take no new in bigamy,
Not my will only, but power, doth withhold;

1 widowhead.— J. R. L.   2 All the early editions read " nurse."
    " Muse." (clearly the true reading) was suggested by the
    Rev. H. Alford in his edition.

Hence comes it that these rhymes, which never had
　Mother, want matter ; and they only have
　A little form, the which their father gave :
They are profane, imperfect, oh ! too bad
　To be counted children of poetry
　Except confirmed and bishopëd by thee.

TO MR. R. W.

If, as mine is, thy life a slumber be,
Seem, when thou read'st these lines, to dream of me ;
Never did Morpheus, nor his brother, wear
Shapes so like those shapes whom they would appear,
As this my letter is like me ; for it
Hath my name, words, hand, feet, heart, mind, and wit ;
It is my deed of gift of me to thee,
It is my will, myself the legacy.
So thy retirings I love, yea, envý,
Bred in thee by a wise meláncholy,
That I rejoice that, unto where thou art,
Though I stay here, I can thus send my heart
As kindly as any enamored patiënt
His picture to his absent love hath sent.

All news I think sooner reach thee than me ;
Havens are heavens, and ships winged angels be
The which both gospel and stern threatenings bring ;
Guiana's harvest is nipped in the spring,

I fear; and with us (methinks) Fate deals so
As with the Jews' guide God did; he did show
Him the rich land, but barred his entry in:
Our slowness is our punishment and sin.
Perchance, these Spanish business[1] being done,
(Which, as the earth between the moon and sun,
Eclipse the light which Guiana would give,)
Our discontinued hopes we shall retrieve :
But if (as all the All must) hopes smoke away
Is not almighty Virtue an India ?

If men be worlds, there is in every one
Something to answer in some proportion
All the world's riches : and in good men this
Virtue our form's form and our soul's soul is.

TO MR. I. L.

Of that short roll of friends writ in my heart,
Which with thy name begins since their depart,
Whether in the English provinces they be,
Or drink of Po, Sequan, or Danuby,
There 's none that sometimes greets us not; and yet
Your Trent is Lethe ; that passed, us you forget.
You do not duties of societies,
If from the embrace of a loved wife you rise,

1 businesses.

View your fat beasts, stretched barns, and laboured fields,
Eat, play, ride, take all joys which all day yields,
And then again to your embracements go ;
Some hours on us your friends, and some bestow
Upon your Muse ; else both we shall repent,
I, that my love, she, that her gifts on you are spent.

TO MR. I. P.

BLEST are your North parts, for all this long time
My sun is with you, cold and dark 's our clime.
Heaven's sun, which stayed so long from us this year,
Stayed in your North (I think) for she was there,
And hither by kind Nature drawn from thence,
Here rages, chafes, and threatens pestilence ;
Yet I, as long as she from hence doth stay
Think this no South, no summer, nor no day.
With thee my kind and unkind heart is run,
There sacrifice it to that beauteous sun :
So may thy pastures with their flowery feasts,
As suddenly as lard, fat thy lean beasts,
So may thy woods oft polled yet ever wear
A green, and (when thee [1] list) a golden hair,
So may all thy sheep bring forth twins, and so
In chase and race may thy horse all out-go,

1 she.

So may thy love and courage ne'er be cold,
Thy son ne'er ward, thy loved wife ne'er seem old,
But may'st thou wish great things and them attain,
As thou tell'st her, and none but her, my pain.

TO THE E. OF D.[1]

WITH SIX HOLY SONNETS.

SEE, Sir, how as the sun's hot masculine flame
    Begets strange creatures on Nile's dirty slime,
    In me your fatherly yet lusty rhyme
(For these songs are their fruits) have wrought the same ;
But though the engendering force from whence they came,
    Be strong enough, and nature do[2] admit
    Seven to be born at once, I send as yet
But six ; they say the seventh hath still some maim ;
    I choose your judgment, which the same degree
    Doth with her sister, your invention, hold,
As fire these drossy rhymes to purify,
    Or as elixir to change them to gold ;
    You are that alchemist which always had
Wit whose one spark could make good things of bad.

1 Earl of Doncaster.　2 doth.

TO SIR H. W.,[1] AT HIS GOING
AMBASSADOR TO VENICE.

AFTER those reverend papers whose soul is
    Our good and great King's loved hand and feared name,
By which to you he derives much of his,
    And (how he may) makes you almost the same,—

A taper of his torch, a copy writ
    From his original, and a fair beam
Of the same warm and dazzling sun, though it
    Must in another sphere his virtue stream;

After those learned papers which your hand
    Hath stored with notes of use and pleasures[2] too,
From which rich treasury you may command
    Fit matter, whether you will write or do;

After those loving papers where[3] friends send,
    With glad grief, to your sea-ward steps farewell,
Which thicken on you now, as prayers ascend
    To heaven in troops at a good man's passing-bell;

Admit this honest paper, and allow
    It such an audience as yourself would ask;
What you must say at Venice, this means now,
    And hath for nature, what you have for task,—

1 Henry Wotton. 2 pleasure. 3 which.

To swear much love, not to be changed before
   Honour alone will to your fortune fit;
Nor shall I then honour your fortune more
   Than I have done your honour wanting it.[1]

But 't is an easier load (though both oppress)
   To want than govern greatness; for we are
In that our own and only business;
   In this, we must for others' vices care.

'T is therefore well your spirits now are placed
   In their last furnace, in activity,
Which fits them (schools and courts and wars o'erpast)
   To touch and test[2] in any best degree.

For me (if there be such a thing as I),
   Fortune (if there be such a thing as she)
Spies that I bear so well her tyranny,
   That she thinks nothing else so fit for me.

But though she part us, to hear my oft prayers
   For your increase God is as near me here;
And to send you what I shall beg his stairs
   In length and ease are alike everywhere.

        1 noble-wanting-wit. 2 taste, 1669.

TO MRS. M. H.

Mad paper, stay, and grudge not here to burn
    With all those sons whom my [1] brain did create;
At least lie hid with me till thou return
    To rags again which is thy native state.

What though thou have enough unworthiness
    To come unto great place as others do,
That's much; emboldens, pulls, thrusts, I confess;
    But 't is not all, thou should'st be wicked too.

And that thou canst not learn, or not of me;
    Yet thou wilt go; go, since thou goest to her
Who lacks but faults to be a prince, for she
    Truth, whom they dare not pardon, dares prefer.

But when thou com'st to that perplexing eye
    Which equally claims love and reverence,
Thou wilt not long dispute it, thou wilt die,
    And, having little now, have then no sense.

Yet when her warm redeeming hand (which is
    A miracle, and made such to work more)
Doth touch thee (sapless leaf) thou grow'st by this
    Her creature, glorified more than before.

[1] thy.

Then, as a mother which delights to hear
  Her early child misspeak half-uttered words,
Or, because majesty doth never fear
  Ill or bold speech, she audience affords.

And then, cold speechless wretch, thou diest again,
  And wisely; what discourse is left for thee?
For [1] speech of ill and her thou must abstain,
  And is there any good which is not she?

Yet may'st thou praise her servants, though not her;
  And Wit and Virtue and Honour her attend;
And since they 're but her clothes, thou shalt not err
  If thou her shape and beauty and grace commend.

Who knows thy destiny? when thou hast done,
  Perchance her cabinet may harbour thee,
Whither all noble ambitious wits do run,
  A nest almost as full of good as she.

When thou art there, if any whom we know
  Were saved before and did that heaven partake,
When she revolves his papers, mark what show
  Of favour she, alone, to them doth make.

Mark if, to get them, she o'erskip the rest;
  Mark if she read them twice, or kiss the name;
Mark if she do the same that they protest;
  Mark if she mark whether [2] her woman came.

1 From. 2 whither.

Mark if slight things be objected and o'erblown :
Mark if her oaths against him be not still
Reserved, and that she grieves she 's not her own,
And chides the doctrine that denies free-will.

I bid thee not do this to be my spy,
Nor to make myself her familiär ;
But so much I do love her choice that I
Would fain love him that shall be loved of her.

TO THE COUNTESS OF BEDFORD.

Honour is so sublime perfection,
And so refined, that when God was alone
And creatureless at first, himself had none ;

But as of the elements these which we tread,
Produce all things with which we 're joyed or fed,
And those are barren both above our head,

So from low persons doth all honour flow ;
Kings, whom they would have honoured, to us show,
And but direct our honour, not bestow.

For when from herbs the pure part must be won
From gross by stilling, this is better done
By despised dung than by the fire or [1] sun.

1 of, 1635, '39. '49, '54.

Care not then, Madam, how low your praises lie ;
In labourers' ballads oft more piety
God finds than in *Te Deums'* melody,

And ordnance raised on towers so many mile
Send not their voice, nor last so long a while,
As fires from th' earth's low vaults in Sicil isle.

Should I say I lived darker than were true,
Your radiation can all clouds subdue
But one ; 't is best light to contemplate you,—

You, for whose body God made better clay,
Or took soul's stuff such as shall late decay,
Or such as needs small change at the last day.

This, as an amber drop enwraps a bee,
Covering discovers [1] your quick soul, that we
May in your through-shine front our heart's thoughts see.

You teach (though we learn not) a thing unknown
To our late times, the use of specular stone,
Through which all things within without were shown.

Of such were temples ; so, and such you are ;
Being and seeming is your equal care ;
And Virtue's whole sum is but Know and Dare. [2]

But as our souls of growth and souls of sense
Have birthright of our reason's soul, yet hence
They fly not from that, nor seek precedence,

1 Coverings discover, 1669. 2 The stanza beginning "Discretion is . . . "
follows this in all editions after that of 1633.

Nature's first lesson, so discretiön,
Must not grudge zeal a place, nor yet keep none,
Not banish itself nor religiön.

Discretion is a wiseman's soul, and so
Religion is a Christian's, and you know
How these are one; her *yea* is not her *no*.

Nor may we hope to solder still and knit
These two, and dare to break them; nor must wit
Be colleague to religion, but be it.

In those poor types of God, round circles, so
Religion's types, the pieceless centers, flow,
And are in all the lines which all ways go.

If either ever wrought in you alone,
Or principally, then religiön
Wrought your ends, and your ways discretiön.

Go thither still, go the same way you went;
Whoso would change, do [1] covet or repent;
Neither can reach you, great and innocent.

TO THE COUNTESS OF HUNTINGDON.
1635.

THAT unripe side of earth, that heavy clime
That gives us man [2] up now, like Adam's time
Before he ate, man's shape, that would yet be
(Knew they not it, and feared beasts' company)

---

[1] doth, 1669.   [2] men (?).

So naked at this day as though man there
From paradise so great a distance were
As yet the news could not arrivëd be
Of Adam's tasting the forbidden tree,
Deprived of that free state which they were in,
And wanting the reward, yet bear the sin.

But, as from extreme heights who downward looks,
Sees men at children's shapes, rivers at brooks',
And loseth younger forms, so to your eye
These, Madam, that without your distance lie,
Must either mist or nothing seem to be,
Who are at home but wit's mere *Atomi.*
But I, who can behold them move and stay,
Have found myself to you just their midway,
And now must pity them; for as they do
Seem sick to me, just so must I to you;
Yet neither will I vex your eyes to see
A sighing ode, nor cross-armed elegy.
I come not to call pity from your heart,
Like some white-livered dotard that would part
Else from his slippery soul with a faint groan,
And faithfully (without you smiled[1]) were gone.
I cannot feel the tempest of a frown,
I may be raised by love, but not thrown down;
Though I can pity those sigh twice a day,
I hate that thing whispers itself away.
Yet since all love is fever,[2] who to trees
Doth talk, doth yet [3] in love's cold ague freeze.
'T is love, but with such fatal weakness made,
That it destroys itself with its own shade.

1 your smile, 1669.   2 feverish, *ibid.*   3 yet doth, *ibid.*

Who first looked sad, grieved, pined and showed his pain,
Was he that first taught women to disdain.
As all things were one [1] nothing dull and weak
Until this raw disordered heap did break,
And several desires led parts away,
Water declined with earth, the air did stay,
Fire rose, and each from other but untied,
Themselves unprisoned were and purified,
So was love first in vast confusion hid,
An unripe willingness which nothing did,
A thirst, an appetite which had no ease,
That found a want, but knew not what would please.
What pretty innocence in those days [2] moved!
Man ignorantly walked by her he loved;
Both sighed and interchanged a speaking eye,
Both trembled and were sick, both [3] knew not why.
That natural fearfulness that struck man dumb,
Might well (those times considered) man become.
As all discoverers, whose first essay
Finds but the place, after, the nearest way,
So passion is to woman's love about,
Nay, farther off, than when we first set out.
It is not love that sueth or doth contend;
Love either conquers, or but meets a friend.
Man's better part consists of purer fire,
And finds itself allowed ere it desire.
Love is wise here, keeps home, gives reason sway,
And journeys not till it find summer-way.

---

[1] were but one, 1669. [2] in that day, *ibid.* [3] yet, *ibid.*

A weather-beaten lover, but once known,
Is sport for every girl to practise on.
Who strives through woman's scorns women to know,
Is lost, and seeks his shadow to outgo.
It must be sickness,[1] after one disdain,
Though he be called aloud, to look again.
Let others sin and grieve ; one cunning sleight
Shall freeze my love to crystal in a night.
I can love first, and (if I win) love still,
And cannot be removed, unless she will.
It is her fault, if I unsure remain ;
She only can untie, I bind again.
The honesties of love with ease I do,
But am no porter for a tedious woe.

But, Madam, I now think on you ; and here,
Where we are at our heights, you but appear ;
We are but clouds you rise from, our noon-ray
But a foul shadow not your break of day.
You are at first hand all that 's fair and right,
And others' good reflects but back your light.
You are a perfectness so curious hit
That youngest flatteries do scandal it ;
For what is more doth what you are restrain,
And though beyond is down the hill again.
We have no next way to you, we cross to 't ;
You are the straight line, thing praised, attribute ;
Each good in you 's a light ; so, many a shade
You make, and in them are your motions made.

---

1 It is mere sickness, 1669.

These are your pictures to the life.   From far
We see you move, and here your zanies are ;
So that no fountain good there is doth grow
In you, but our dim actions faintly show.
    Then find I, if man's noblest part be love,
Your purest lustre must that shadow move.
The soul with body is a heaven combined
With earth, and for man's ease but nearer joined,[1]
Where thoughts the stars of soul we understand,
We guess not their large natures, but command.
And love in you that bounty is of light,
That gives to all and yet hath infinite ;
Whose heat doth force us thither to intend,
But soul we find too earthly to ascend
'Till slow access hath made it wholly pure,
Able immortal clearness to endure.
Who dare aspire this journey with a stain,
Hath weight will force him headlong back again ;
No more can impure man retain and move
In that pure region of a worthy love,
Than earthly substance can unforced aspire,
And leave his nature to converse with fire.
    Such may have eye and hand, may sigh, may speak,
But like swoln bubbles, when they are highest, they
        break.
Though far removèd Northern fleets[2] scarce find
The sun's comfort, others[3] think him too kind.
There is an equal distance from her eye ;

1 man's ease nearer joined, 1649, '54, '69.   2 isles, 1669.
3 yet some, *ibid.*

Men perish too far-off, and burn too nigh.
But as air takes the sunbeams equal-bright
From the first rays [1] to his last opposite,
So able [2] man, blest with a virtuous love;
Remote or near, or howsoe'er they move,
There [3] virtue breaks all clouds, that might annoy;
There is no emptiness, but all is joy.
He much profanes (whom valiant heats do move)
To style his wandering rage of passion *love*.
Love, that imparts [4] in every thing delight,
Is fancied in the soul, not in the sight; [5]
Why love among the virtues is not known,
Is, that love is them all contracted one. [6]

A DIALOGUE BETWEEN SIR HENRY WOTTON AND MR. DONNE.

1635.

IF her disdain least change in you can move,
    You do not love;
For when the [7] hope gives fuel to the fire,
    You sell desire.
Love is not love, but given free;
And so is mine, so should yours be.

1 rays first, 1669. 2 happy, *ibid.* 3 Their, *ibid.* 4 imports, *ibid.*
 5 "Is fancied" is all that is given of this verse in the editions
of 1635, '39; the reading adopted is that of 1649. Is fancied by
the soul, not appetite, 1669. 6 Contract in one, 1649, '54, '69.
 7 that, 1669.

II.—4*

Her heart, that melts to hear of others' moan,
                    To mine is stone;
Her eyes, that weep a stranger's eyes to see,
                    Joy to wound me:
          Yet I so well affect each part,
          As (caused by them) I love my smart.

Say her disdainings justly must be graced
                    With name of chaste;
And that she frowns lest longing should exceed
                    And raging breed;
          So her disdains can ne'er offend,
          Unless self-love take private end.

'T is love breeds love in me, and cold disdain
                    Kills that again,
As water causeth fire to fret and fume
                    Till all consume.
          Who can of love more gift make [1]
          Than to love self for Love's sake?

I 'll never dig in quarry of an heart,
                    To have no part;
Nor rest[2] in fiery eyes which always are
                    Canicular.
          Who this way would a lover prove,
          May show his patience, not his love.

[1] Who can of love more rich gift make,
   Than to love self-love for love's sake? 1649, '54.
   Who can of love more rich gift make,
   Than to Love's self for love's own sake? 1669.
[2] Nor roast, *ibid.*

A frown may be sometimes for physic good,
    But not for food;
And for that raging humour there is sure
    A gentler cure.
Why bar you love of private end,
Which never should to public tend?

TO THE COUNTESS OF BEDFORD.

BEGUN IN FRANCE, BUT NEVER PERFECTED.

THOUGH I be dead and buried, yet I have
(Living in you) Court enough in my grave,
As oft as there I think myself to be,
So many resurrections waken me;
That thankfulness your favours have begot
In me, embalms me that I do not rot:
This season, as 't is Easter, as 't is spring,
Must both to growth and to confession bring
My thoughts disposed unto your influence; so
These verses bud, so these confessions grow;
First I confess I have to others lent
Your stock and over-prodigally spent
Your treasure, for since I had never known
Virtue or [1] beauty, but as they are grown
In you, I should not think or say they shine
(So as I have) in any other mine;
Next I confess this my confession;

1 and, 1649, '54, '69.

For 't is some fault thus much to touch upon
Your praise to you, where half-rights seem too much
And make your mind's sincere complexion blush.
Next I confess my impenitence; for I
Can scarce repent my first fault, since thereby
Remote low spirits, which shall ne'er read you,
May in less lessons find enough to do,
By studying copies, not originals;
   Desunt cetera.

A LETTER TO THE LADY CAREY, AND MRS. ESSEX RICHE, FROM AMIENS.

MADAM,
HERE, where by all all saints invokëd are,
'T were too much schism to be singular,
And 'gainst a practice general to war.

Yet turning to saints, should my humility
To other saint than you directed be,
That were to make my schism heresy.

Nor would I be a convertite so cold
As not to tell it; if this be too bold,
Pardons are in this market cheaply sold.

Where, because faith is in too low degree,
I thought it some apostleship in me
To speak things which by faith alone I see;

That is, of you, who is [1] a firmament
Of virtues where no one is grown or spent ;
They 're your materials, not your ornament.

Others whom we call virtuous are not so
In their whole substance ; but their virtues grow
But in their humours, and at seasons show.

For when through tasteless flat humility [2]
In dough-baked men some harmlessness we see,
'T is but his phlegm that 's virtuous, and not he :

So is the blood sometimes ; whoever ran
To danger unimportuned, he was than
No better than a sanguine-virtuous man.

So cloisteral men, who, in pretence of fear,
All contributions to this life forbear,
Have virtue in melancholy, and only there.

Spiritual choleric critics, which in all
Religions find faults, and forgive no fall,
Have through their [3] zeal virtue but in their gall.

We are thus but parcel-gilt ; to gold we are grown,
When virtue is our soul's complexiön ;
Who knows his virtue's name or place, hath none.

Virtue is but aguish,[4] when 't is several,
By occasion waked and circumstantiäl ;
True Virtue is soul, always in all deeds All.

1 are.　2 humidity, 1669.　3 this.　4 anguish, 1649, '54.

This Virtue thinking to give dignity
To your soul, found there no infirmity;
For your soul was as good virtúe as she.

She therefore wrought upon that part of you
Which is scarce less than soul, as she could do,
And so hath made your beauty virtue too.

Hence comes it that your beauty wounds not hearts,
As others', with profane and sensual darts,
But as an influence virtuous thoughts imparts.

But if such friends by the honour of your sight
Grow capable of this so great a light
As to partake your virtues and their might,

What must I think that influence must do
Where it finds sympathy and matter too,
Virtue and beauty of the same stuff as you,

Which is your noble worthy sister? she
Of whom, if what in this my ecstasy
And revelation of you both I see,

I should write here (as in short galleries
The master at the end large glasses ties,
So to present the room twice to our eyes),

So I should give this letter length, and say
That which I said of you; there is no way
From either, but by [1] the other, not to stray.

1 to, 1669.

May therefore this be enough to testify
My true devotion free from flattery;
He that believes himself, doth never lie.

TO THE COUNTESS OF SALISBURY.

AUGUST, 1614.

FAIR, great, and good, since seeing you we see
What Heaven can do, and [1] what any earth can be;
Since now your beauty shines, now, when the sun,
Grown stale, is to so low a value run
That his dishevelled beams and scattered fires
Serve but for ladies' periwigs and tires
In lovers' sonnets, you come to repair
God's book of creatures, teaching what is fair;
Since now, when all is withered, shrunk, and dried,
All virtues ebbed out to a dead low tide,
All the world's frame being crumbled into sand
Where every man thinks by himself to stand,
Integrity, friendship, and confidence
(Cements of greatness) being vapoured hence
And narrow man being filled with little shares,
Court,[2] city, church, are all shops of small-wares,
All having blown to sparks their noble fire
And drawn their sound gold ingot into wire,
All trying by a love of littleness
To make abridgments and to draw to less

1 can do, what any, 1635, '39, '49, '54. 2 Courts, 1669.

Even that nothing which at first we were,
Since in these times your greatness doth appear,
And that we learn by it that man, to get
Towards Him that 's infinite, must first be great;
Since in an age so ill, as none is fit
So much as to accuse, much less mend it,
(For who can judge or witness of those times,
Where all alike are guilty of the crimes?)
Where he that would be good is thought by all
A monster, or at best fantastical,
Since now you durst be good, and that I do
Discern, by daring to contemplate you,
That there may be degrees of fair, great, good,
Through your light,[1] largeness, virtue, understood,
If, in this sacrifice of mine, be shown
Any small spark of these, call it your own,
And if things like these have been said by me
Of others, call not that idolatry,
For had God made man first, and man had seen
The third day's fruits and flowers and various green,
He might have said the best that he could say
Of those fair creatures which were made that day,
And when next day he had admired the birth
Of sun, moon, stars, fairer than late praised earth,
He might have said the best that he could say,
And not be chid for praising yesterday,
So, though some things are not together true,
As, that another is worthiest, and that you,

1 lights, 1669.

Yet to say so doth not condemn a man,
If, when he spoke them, they were both true than.
How fair a proof of this in our soul grows!
We first have souls of growth and sense, and those,
When our last soul, our soul immortal, came,
Were swallowed into it and have no name;
Nor doth he injure those souls, which doth cast
The power and praise of both them on the last;
No more do I wrong any; I adore[1]
The same things now which I adored before,
The subject changed and measure; the same thing
In a low constable and in the king
I reverence,—his power to work on me;
So did I humbly reverence each degree
Of fair, great, good; but more, now I am come
From having found their walks, to find their home.
And, as I owe my first souls thanks, that they
For my last soul did fit and mould my clay,
So am I debtor unto them whose worth
Enabled me to profit, and take forth
This new great lesson, thus to study you,
Which none, not reading others first, could do.
Nor lack I light to read this book, though I
In a dark cave, yea, in a grave do lie;
For, as your fellow-angels, so you do
Illustrate them who come to study you.
The first whom we in histories do find
To have professed all arts, was one born blind:

1 if I adore.

He lacked those eyes beasts have as well as we,
Not those by which angels are seen and see ;
So, though I 'm born without those eyes to live,
Which Fortune, who hath none herself, doth give,
Which are fit means to see bright courts and you,
Yet, may I see you thus, as now I do,
I shall by that all goodness have discerned,
And, though I burn my library, be learned.

TO [1] THE LADY BEDFORD.

You that are she and you, that 's double she,
In her dead face half of yourself shall see ;
She was the other part ; for so they do,
Which build them friendships, become one of two,[2]
So two, that but themselves no third can fit ;
Which were to be so when they were not yet,
Twins, though their birth Cusco and Musco take,
As divers stars one constellation make,
Paired like two eyes, have equal motion, so
Both but one means to see, one way to go.
Had you died first, a carcase she had been,
And we your rich tomb in her face had seen.
She like the soul is gone, and you here stay,
Not a live friend, but th' other half of clay ;
And since you act that part, as men say, here
Lies such a prince, when but one part is there,

1 Elegy to, 1633. To the Countess of Bedford, 1669.
2 of the two, 1669.

And do all honour and devotion due
Unto the whole, so we all reverence you;
For such a friendship who would not adore
In you, who are all what both was[1] before?
Not all, as if some perishëd by this,
But so, as all in you contracted is;
As of this All, though many parts decay,
The pure, which elemented them, shall stay,
And, though diffused and spread in infinite,
Shall re-collect and in one all unite,
So, Madam, as her soul to heaven is fled,
Her flesh rests in the earth as in the bed,
Her virtues do, as to their proper sphere,
Return to dwell with you, of whom they were;
As perfect motions are all circular,
So they to you, their sea, whence less streams are.
She was all spices, you all metals; so
In you two we did both rich Indies know.
And as no fire nor rust can spend or waste
One dram of gold, but what was first shall last,
Though it be forced in water, earth, salt, air,
Expansed in infinite, none will impair,
So to yourself you may additions take,
But nothing can you less or changëd make.
Seek not, in seeking new, to seem to doubt
That you can match her or not be without;
But let some faithful book in her room be,
Yet, but of Judith, no such book as she.

[1] were.

SAPPHO TO PHILÆNIS.

WHERE is that holy fire which verse is said
To have? is that enchanting force decayed?
Verse, that draws Nature's works [1] from Nature's law,
Thee, her best work, to her work cannot draw.
Have my tears quenched my old poetic fire?
Why quenched they not as well that of desire?
Thoughts, my mind's creatures, often are with thee,
But I, their maker, want their liberty:
Only thine image in my heart doth sit;
But that is wax, and fires environ it.
My fires have driven, thine have drawn it hence,
And I am robbed of picture, heart, and sense.
Dwells with me still mine irksome memory,
Which both to keep and lose grieves equally.
That tells me how fair thou art: thou art so fair,
As gods, when gods to thee I do compare,
Are graced thereby, and to make blind men see
What things gods are, I say they 're like to thee.
For if we justly call each silly man
A little world, what shall we call thee than?
Thou art not soft and clear and straight and fair
As down, as stars, cedars, and lilies are;
But thy right hand and cheek and eye only,
Are like thy other hand and cheek and eye.

1 work, 1649, '54, '69.

Such was my Phao awhile, but shall be never
As thou wast, art, and, oh! mayest [1] be ever!
Here lovers swear in their idolatry
That I am such; but grief discolours me:
And yet I grieve the less, lest grief remove
My beauty and make me unworthy of thy love.
Plays some soft boy with thee? oh! there wants yet
A mutual feeling which should sweeten it.
His chin a thorny hairy unevenness
Doth threaten, and some daily change possess.
Thy body is a natural paradise
In whose self, unmanured, all pleasure lies,
Nor needs perfection; why should'st thou than
Admit the tillage of a harsh rough man?
Men leave behind them that which their sin shows,
And are as thieves traced, which rob when it snows;
But of our dalliance no more signs there are
Than fishes leave in streams or birds in air,
And between us all sweetness may be had,
All, all that nature yields, or art can add.
My two lips, eyes, thighs, differ from thy two
But so as thine from one another do;
And oh! no more; the likeness being such,
Why should they not alike in all parts touch?
Hand to strange hand, lip to lip none denies;
Why should they breast to breast, or thighs to thighs?
Likeness begets such strange self-flattery
That touching myself, all seems done to thee.

[1] may'st thou be.

Myself I embrace, and mine own hands I kiss,
And amorously thank myself for this.
Me in my glass I call thee ; but, alas !
When I would kiss, tears dim mine eyes and glass.
O, cure this loving madness and restore
Me to me, thee[1] my half, my all, my more.
So may thy cheek's red outwear scarlet dye,
And their white, whiteness of the Galaxy;
So may thy mighty amazing beauty move
Envy in all women and in all men love ;
And so be change and sickness far from thee,
As thou, by coming near, keep'st them from me.

TO BEN JONSON,

9 NOVEMBRIS, 1603.

1635.

IF great men wrong me, I will spare myself;
If mean, I will spare them; I know the pelf
Which is ill got, the owner doth upbraid ;
It may corrupt a judge, make me afraid,
And a jury: but 't will revenge in this,
That, though himself be judge, he guilty is.
What care I though of weakness men tax me?
I had rather sufferer than doer be;

[1] shee, 1633.

That I did trust, it was my nature's praise,
For breach of word I knew but as a phrase.
That judgment is, that surely can comprise
The world in precepts, most happy and most wise.
What though? though less, yet some of both have we,
Who have learned it by use and misery.
Poor I, whom every petty cross doth trouble,
Who apprehend each hurt that 's done me double,
Am of this (though it should sink me) careless,
It would but force me to a stricter goodness.
They have great gain of me, who gain do win
(If such gain be not loss) from every sin.
The standing of great men's lives would afford
A pretty sum, if God would sell his word.
He cannot; they can theirs, and break them too.
How unlike they are that they are likened to!
Yet I conclude they are amidst my evils,
If good, like gods, the naught are so like devils.

TO SIR THOMAS ROWE, 1603.

1635.

DEAR TOM,
TELL her, if she to hired servants show
Dislike, before they take their leave they go,
When nobler spirits start at no disgrace;
For who hath but one mind, hath but one face.

If then why I take not my leave she ask,
Ask her again why she did not unmask.
Was she or proud or cruel, or knew she
'T would make my loss more felt, and pitied me?
Or did she fear one kiss might stay for moe?
Or else was she unwilling I should go?
I think the best and love so faithfully
I cannot choose but think that she loves me.
If this prove not my faith, then let her try
How in her service I would fructify.
Ladies have boldly loved; bid her renew
That decayed worth and prove the times past true.
Then he, whose wit and verse grows now so lame,
With songs to her will the wild Irish tame.
Howe'er, I 'll wear the black and white ribánd;
White for her fortunes, black for mine shall stand.
I do esteem her favour, not the stuff;
If what I have was given, I have enough,
And all 's well, for had she loved, I had not had
All my friends' hate; for now departing sad
I feel not that: yet as the rack the gout
Cures, so hath *this* worse grief *that* quite put out:
My first disease nought but that worse cureth,
Which (I dare fóresay) nothing cures but death.
Tell her all this before I am forgot,
That not too late she grieve she loved me not.
    Burdened with this, I was to depart less
    Willing than those which die and not confess.

FUNERAL ELEGIES.

FUNERAL ELEGIES.

AN ANATOMY OF THE WORLD.

WHEREIN, BY OCCASION OF THE UNTIMELY DEATH OF
MISTRESS ELIZABETH DRURY,
THE FRAILTY AND THE DECAY OF THIS WHOLE WORLD IS
REPRESENTED.

TO THE PRAISE OF THE DEAD AND THE ANATOMY.[1]

WELL died the World, that we might live to see
This world of wit in his Anatomy:
No evil wants his good ; so wilder heirs
Bedew their fathers' tombs with forcëd tears,
Whose state requites their loss : whiles thus we gain,
Well may we walk in blacks, but not complain.
Yet how can I consent the World is dead
While this Muse lives, which in his spirit's stead
Seems to inform a world, and bids it be
In spite of loss or frail mortality?
And thou the subject of this well-born thought,
Thrice-noble maid, could'st not have found nor sought
A fitter time to yield to thy sad fate,
Than whiles this spirit lives that can relate
Thy worth so well to our last nephews' eyne
That they shall wonder both at his and thine :

1 Probably by Bishop Hall.

71

Admired match, where strives in mutual grace
The cunning pencil and the comely face!
A task, which thy fair goodness made too much
For the bold pride of vulgar pens to touch :
Enough is us [1] to praise them that praise thee,
And say that but enough those praises be,
Which, had'st thou lived, had hid their fearful head
From th' angry checkings of thy modest red :
Death bars reward and shame ; when envy's gone,
And gain, 't is safe to give the dead their own.
As then the wise Egyptians wont to lay
More on their tombs than houses (these of clay,
But those of brass or marble were), so we
Give more unto thy ghost than unto thee.
Yet what we give to thee, thou gav'st to us,
And may'st but thank thyself for being thus :
Yet what thou gav'st and wert, O happy maid,
Thy grace professed all due, where 't is repaid.
So these high songs, that to thee suited bin,
Serve but to sound thy Maker's praise and thine,
Which thy dear soul as sweetly sings to him
Amid the choir of saints and seraphim,
As any angel's tongue [2] can sing of thee ;
The subjects differ, though the skill agree :
For as by infant years men judge of age,
Thy early love, thy virtues, did presage
What high part thou bear'st in those best of songs
Whereto no burden nor no end belongs.
Sing on, thou virgin soul, whose lossful gain
Thy love-sick parents have bewailed in vain ;
Never may thy name be in our songs forgot,[3]
Till we shall sing thy ditty and thy note.

1 it is, 1669. 2 angels' tongues, *ibid.* 3 be in songs forgot, *ibid.*

AN ANATOMY OF THE WORLD.

THE FIRST ANNIVERSARY.

WHEN that rich soul which to her heaven is gone,
Who [1] all do celebrate who know they have one,
(For who is sure he hath a soul, unless
It see and judge and follow worthiness,
And by deeds praise it? he who doth not this,
May lodge an inmate soul, but 't is not his,)
When that queen ended here her progress-time,
And as to her standing-house to heaven did climb,
Where, loath to make the saints attend her long,
She 's now a part both of the choir and song,
This world in that great earthquake languishëd;
For in a common bath of tears it bled,
Which drew the strongest vital spirits out;
But succoured then [2] with a perplexëd doubt,—
Whether the world did lose or gain in this,
(Because, since now no other way there is
But goodness, to see her whom all would see,
All must endeavour to be good as she,)
This great consumption to a fever turned,
And so the world had fits; it joyed, it mourned;
And, as men think that agues physic are,
And th' ague being spent, give over care,
So thou, sick world, mistak'st thyself to be
Well, when, alas, thou 'rt in a lethargy:

1 Whom. 2 them, 1649, '54, '69.

Her death did wound and tame thee than, and than
Thou might'st have better spared the sun or man ;
That wound was deep ; but 't is more misery
That thou hast lost thy sense and memory.
'T was heavy then to hear thy voice of moan,
But this is worse, that thou art speechless grown.
Thou hast forgot thy name thou hadst ; thou wast
Nothing but she, and her thou hast o'erpast.
For as a child kept from the fount until
A prince, expected long, come to fulfil
The ceremonies, thou unnamed hadst laid,
Had not her coming thee her palace made :
Her name defined thee, gave thee form and frame,
And thou forget'st to celebrate thy name.
Some months she hath been dead (but being dead,
Measures of time are all determinëd)
But long she hath been away, long, long : yet none
Offers to tell us who it is that 's gone ;
But as in states doubtful of future heirs,
When sickness without remedy impairs
The present prince, they 're loath it should be said
The prince doth languish, or the prince is dead,
So mankind, feeling now a general thaw,
A strong example gone, equal to law,
The cément, which did faithfully compact
And glue[1] all virtues, now resolved and slacked,
Thought it some blasphemy to say she was dead
Or that our weakness was discoverëd

1 give, 1649, '54, '69.

In that confession, therefore spoke no more
Than tongues, the soul being gone, the loss deplore.
But, though it be too late to succour thee,
Sick world, yea, dead, yea, putrefied, since she,
Thy intrinsic balm and thy preservative,
Can never be renewed, thou never live,
I (since no man can make thee live) will try
What we may gain by thy Anatomy.
Her death hath taught us dearly that thou art
Corrupt and mortal in thy purest part.
Let no man say, the world itself being dead,
'T is labour lost to have discoverèd
The world's infirmities, since there is none
Alive to study this dissectiön,
For there 's a kind of world remaining still;
Though she, which did inanimate and fill
The world, be gone, yet in this last long night
Her ghost doth walk, that is, a glimmering light,
A faint weak love of virtue and of good
Reflects from her on them which understood
Her worth ; and though she have shut in all day,
The twilight of her memory doth stay,
Which, from the carcase of the old world free,
Creates a new world, and new creatures be
Produced: the matter and the stuff of this
Her virtue, and the form our practice is :
And though [1] to be thus elemented arm
These creatures from home-born intrinsic harm,

1 thought, 1633.

(For all assumed unto this dignity,
So many weedless paradises be,
Which of themselves produce no venomous sin,
Except some foreign serpent bring it in,)
Yet, because outward storms the strongest break,
And strength itself by confidence grows weak,
This new world may be safer, being told

The sickness of the world.* The dangers and diseases of the old;
For with due temper men do then[1] forego
Or covet things, when they their true worth know.

Impossibility of health. There is no health; physicians say that we
At best enjoy but a neutrality;
And can there be worse sickness than to know
That we are never well, nor can be so?
We are born ruinous: poor mothers cry
That children come not right nor orderly
Except they headlong come and fall upon
An ominous precipitatiön.
How witty's ruin, how importunate
Upon mankind! it laboured to frustrate
Even God's purpose, and made woman, sent
For man's relief, cause of his languishment;
They were to good ends, and they are so still,
But accessory and principal in ill;
For that first marriage was our funeral;
One woman at one blow then killed us all,
And singly, one by one, they kill us now.
We do delightfully ourselves allow

---

1 them, 1649, '54, '69.
* These side-notes are found only in the edition of 1633.

To that consumption, and, profusely blind,
We kill ourselves to propagate our kind;
And yet we do not that; we are not men:
There is not now that mankind which was then
When as the sun and man did seem to strive
(Joint-tenants of the world) who should survive, *Shortness*
When stag and raven and the long-lived tree, *of life.*
Compared with man, died in minority,
When, if a slow-paced star had stolen away
From the observer's marking, he might stay
Two or three hundred years to see 't again,
And then make up his observation plain;
When, as the age was long, the size was great;
Man's growth confessed and recompensed the meat,
So spacïous and large, that every soul
Did a fair kingdom and large realm control,
And when the very stature thus erect
Did that soul a good way towards heaven direct.
Where is this mankind now? who lives to age
Fit to be made Methusalem his page?
Alas! we scarce live long enough to try
Whether a true-made clock run right or lie.
Old grandsires talk of yesterday with sorrow,
And for our children we reserve to-morrow.
So short is life, that every peasant strives
In a torn house or field to have three lives.
And as in lasting, so in length is man,
Contracted to an inch, who was a span; *Smallness of*
For had a man at first in forests strayed *stature.*
Or shipwracked in the sea, one would have laid

A wager that an elephant or whale
That met him, would not hastily assail
A thing so equal to him; now alas!
The fairies and the pigmies well may pass
As credible; mankind decays so soon,
We are scarce our fathers' shadows cast at noon:
Only death adds t' our length, nor are we grown
In stature to be men, till we are none.
But this were light, did our less volume hold
All the old text, or had we changed to gold
Their silver, or disposed into less glass
Spirits of virtue which then scattered was:
But 't is not so: we 're not retired but damped,
And, as our bodies, so our minds are cramped:
'T is shrinking, not close weaving, that hath thus
In mind and body both bedwarfëd us.
We seem ambitious God's whole work t' undo;
Of nothing he made us, and we strive, too,
To bring ourselves to nothing back; and we
Do what we can to do 't so soon as he:
With new diseases on ourselves we war,
And with new physic, a worse engine far.
This [1] man, this world's vice-emperor, in whom
All faculties, all graces are at home,
(And if in other creatures they appear,
They 're but man's ministers and legates there,
To work on their rebellions and reduce
Them to civility and to man's use;)
This man, whom God did woo, and, loath t' attend
Till man came up, did down to man descend,

[1] Thus, 1633.

This man so great that all that is is his,
Oh what a trifle and poor thing he is!
If man were any thing, he 's nothing now;
Help, or at least some time to waste, allow
T' his other wants, yet when he did depart
With her whom we lament, he lost his heart.
She, of whom th' ancients seemed to prophesy
When they called virtues by the name of *she*,
She, in whom virtue was so much refined,
That for alloy unto so pure a mind
She took the weaker sex, she, that could drive
The poisonous tincture and the stain of Eve
Out of her thoughts and deeds, and purify
All by a true religious alchemy,
She, she is dead; she 's dead: when thou knowest this,
Thou knowest how poor a trifling thing man is,
And learn'st thus much by our Anatomy,
The heart being perished, no part can be free,
And that, except thou feed (not banquet) on
The supernatural food, religiön,
Thy better growth grows witheréd and scant;
Be more than man, or thou 'rt less than an ant.
Then as mankind, so is the world's whole frame
Quite out of joint, almost created lame:
For before God had made up all the rest,
Corruption entered and depraved the best;
It seized the Angels, and then first of all
The world did in her cradle take a fall
And turned her brains and took a general maim,
Wronging each joint of th' universal frame.

The noblest part, man, felt it first; and than
Both beasts and plants, cursed in the curse of man.

Decay of na-
ture in other
parts.
So did the world from the first hour decay
That evening was beginning of the day;
And now the springs and summers which we see,
Like sons of women after fifty be.
And new philosophy calls all in doubt ;
The element of fire is quite put out ;
The sun is lost, and th' earth, and no man's wit
Can well direct him where to look for it.
And freely men confess that this world 's spent,
When in the planets and the firmament
They seek so many new ; they see that this
Is crumbled out again to his atomies.
'T is all in pieces, all coherence gone,
All just supply, and all relatïon :
Prince, subject, father, son, are things forgot,
For every man alone thinks he hath got
To be a phœnix, and that then can be
None of that kind of which he is, but he.
This is the world's condition now, and now
She, that should all parts to reunion bow,
She, that had all magnetic force alone
To draw and fasten sundered parts in one,
She, whom wise nature had invented then
When she observed that every sort of men
Did in their voyäge in this world's sea stray
And needed a new compass for their way,
She, that was best and first original
Of all fair copies, and the general

Steward to fate, she, whose rich eyes and breast
Gilt the West-Indies, and perfumed the East,
Whose having breathed in this world did bestow
Spice on those isles, and bade them still smell so,
And that rich Indie which doth gold inter
Is but as single money coined from her,
She, to whom this world must itself refer
As suburbs, or the microcosm of her,
She, she is dead; she 's dead : when thou knowest this
Thou knowest how lame a cripple this world is,
And learn'st thus much by our Anatomy,
That this world's general sickness doth not lie
In any humour, or one certain part,
But, as thou sawest it rotten at the heart,
Thou seest a hectic fever hath got hold
Of the whole substance, not to be controlled,
And that thou hast but one way not t' admit
The world's infection, to be none of it.
For the world's subtlest immaterial parts
Feel this consuming wound, and age's darts;
For the world's beauty is decayed or gone,
Beauty, that 's colour and proportiön.
We think the heavens enjoy their spherical,
Their round proportiön, embracing all,
But yet their various and perplexed course,
Observed in divers ages, doth enforce
Men to find out so many eccentric parts,
Such divers downright lines, such overthwarts,
As disproportion that pure form; it tears
The firmament in eight-and-forty shares,

II.— 6

And in these constellations then arise
New stars, and old do vanish from our eyes,
As though heaven suffered earthquakes, peace or war,
When new towers rise and old demolished are.
They have impaled within a zodiac
The free-born sun, and keep twelve signs awake
To watch his steps; the Goat and Crab control
And fright him back, who else to either pole
(Did not these Tropics fetter him) might run;
For his course is not round, nor can the sun
Perfect a circle, or maintain his way
One inch direct, but where he rose to-day
He comes no more, but with a cozening line,
Steals by that point and so is serpentine,
And seeming weary with [1] his reeling thus,
He means to sleep, being now fallen nearer us.
So of the stars which boast that they do run
In circle still, none ends where he begun:
All their proportion 's lame, it sinks, it swells;
For of meridians and parallels
Man hath weaved out a net and this net thrown
Upon the heavens, and now they are his own.
Loath to go up the hill, or labour thus
To go to heaven, we make heaven come to us;
We spur, we rein the stars, and in their race
They 're diversely content t' obey our pace. [2]
But keeps the earth her round proportion still?
Doth not a Tenarus or higher hill

1 of.   2 peace, 1633.

Rise so high like a rock, that one might think
The floating moon would shipwrack there and sink?
Seas are so deep, that whales being struck to-day,
Perchance to-morrow scarce at middle way
Of their wished journey's end, the bottom, die :
And men, to sound depths, so much line untie,
As one might justly think that there would rise
At end thereof one of th' antipodies :
If under all a vault infernal be,
(Which sure is spaciöus, except that we
Invent another torment, that there must
Millions into a strait hot room be thrust)
Then solidness and roundness have no place :
Are these but warts and pockholes in the face
Of th' earth? Think so ; but yet confess, in this
The world's proportiön disfigured is,
That those two legs whereon it doth rely,
Reward and punishment, are bent awry :

*Disorder in
the world.*

And, oh ! it can no more be questionëd,
That beauty's best, proportiön, is dead,
Since even grief itself, which now alone
Is left us, is without proportiön.
She, by whose lines proportiön should be
Examined, measure of all symmetry,
Whom had that ancient seen, who thought souls made
Of harmony, he would at next have said
That harmony was she, and thence infer
That souls were but resultances from her
And did from her into our bodies go
As to our eyes the forms from objects flow,

She, who, if those great doctors truly said
That the ark to man's proportïon was made,
Had been a type for that, as that might be
A type of her in this, that contrary
Both elements and passions lived at peace
In her who caused all civil war to cease,
She, after whom what form soe'er we see
Is discord and rude incongruity,
She, she is dead; she 's dead: when thou know'st this,
Thou know'st how ugly a monster this world is,
And learn'st thus much by our Anatomy,
That here is nothing to enamour thee,
And that not only faults in inward parts,
Corruptions in our brains or in our hearts,
Poisoning the fountains whence our actions spring,
Endanger us, but that, if every thing
Be not done fitly and in proportïon
To satisfy wise and good lookers-on,
(Since most men be such as most think they be,)
They 're loathsome too by this deformity.
For Good and Well must in our actions meet;
Wicked is not much worse than indiscreet.
But beauty's other second element,
Colour and lustre, now is as near spent,
And had the world his just proportïon,
Were it a ring still, yet the stone is gone;
As a compassionate turquoise which doth tell,
By looking pale, the wearer is not well,
As gold falls sick, being stung with mercury,
All the world's parts of such complexion be.

When Nature was most busy, the first week,
Swaddling the new-born earth, God seemed to like
That she should sport herself sometimes and play,
To mingle and vary colours every day,
And then, as though she could not make enow,[1]
Himself his various rainbow did allow.
Sight is the noblest sense of any one,
Yet sight hath only colour to feed on,
And colour is decayed; summer's robe grows
Dusky and like an oft-dyed garment shows.
Our blushing red, which used in cheeks to spread,
Is inward sunk, and only our souls are red.
Perchance the world might have recovered,
If she, whom we lament, had not been dead;
But she, in whom all white and red and blue
(Beauty's ingredients) voluntary grew ·
As in an unvexed paradise, from whom
Did all things' verdure and their lustre come,
Whose composition was miraculous,
Being all colour, all diaphanous,
(For air and fire but thick gross bodies were,
And liveliest stones but drowsy and pale to her)
She, she is dead; she 's dead: when thou know'st this,
Thou knowest how wan a ghost this our world is,
And learn'st thus much by our Anatomy,
That it should more affright than pleasure thee,
And that, since all fair colour then did sink,
'T is now but wicked vanity to think
To colour vicious deeds with good pretence,
Or with bought colours to illude men's sense.

1 enough, 1633.

II.—6*

Weakness in the want of correspondence of heaven and earth.

Nor in aught more this world's decay appears,
Than that her influence the heaven forbears,
Or that the elements do not feel this;
The father or the mother barren is;
The clouds conceive not rain, or do not pour,
In the due birth-time, down the balmy shower;
Th' air doth not motherly sit on the earth,
To hatch her seasons and give all things birth;
Spring-times were common cradles, but are tombs,
And false conceptions fill the general wombs;
Th' air shows such meteors as none can see
Not only what they mean, but what they be,
Earth such new worms as would have troubled much
Th' Egyptian Mages to have made more such.
What artist now dares boast that he can bring
Heaven hither, or constellate any thing,
So as the influence of those stars may be
Imprisoned in an herb, or charm, or tree,
And do by touch all which those stars could do?
The art is lost, and correspondence too;
For heaven gives little, and the earth takes less,
And man least knows their trade and purposes.
If this commérce 'twixt heaven and earth were not
Embarred, and all this traffic quite forgot,
She, for whose loss we have lamented thus,
Would work more fully and powerfully on us;
Since herbs and roots by dying lose not all,
But they, yea ashes too, are médicinal,
Death could not quench her virtue so but that
It would be (if not followed) wondered at,

And all the world would be one dying swan
To sing her funeral praise and vanish than.
But as some serpents' poison hurteth not
Except it be from the live serpent shot,
So doth her virtue need her here to fit
That unto us, she working more than it.
But she, in whom to such maturity
Virtue was grown past growth, that it must die,
She, from whose influence all impression came,
But by receiver's impotences lame,
Who, though she could not transubstantiate
All states to gold, yet gilded every state,
So that some princes have some temperance,
Some counsellors some purpose to advance
The common profit, and some people have
Some stay, no more than kings should give, to crave,
Some women have some taciturnity,
Some nunneries some grains of chastity,
She, that did thus much, and much more could do,
But that our age was iron, and rusty too,
She, she is dead; she 's dead: when thou know'st this,
Thou know'st how dry a cinder this world is,
And learn'st thus much by our Anatomy,
That 't is in vain to dew or mollify
It with thy tears, or sweat, or blood: nothing
Is worth our travail, grief, or perishing,
But those rich joys which did possess her heart,
Of which she 's now partaker and a part.
But, as in cutting up a man that 's dead,　　*Conclusion.*
The body will not last out to have read

On every part, and therefore men direct
Their speech to parts that are of most effect,
So the world's carcase would not last, if I
Were punctual in this Anatomy,
Nor smells it well to hearers if one tell
Them their disease, who fain would think they 're well.
Here therefore be the end; and, blessed maid,
Of whom is meant whatever hath been said
Or shall be spoken well by any tongue,
Whose name refines coarse lines and makes prose song,
Accept this tribute, and his first year's rent,
Who, till his dark short taper's end be spent,
As oft as thy feast sees this widowed earth,
Will yearly celebrate thy second birth,
That is, thy death; for though the soul of man
Be got when man is made, 't is born but than
When man doth die; our body 's as the womb,
And, as a midwife, death directs it home;
And you her creatures, whom she works upon,
And have your last and best concoctiön
From her example and her virtue, if you
In reverence to her do think it due
That no one should her praises thus rehearse,
As matter fit for chronicle, not verse,
Vouchsafe to call to mind that God did make
A last and lasting'st piece, a song.   He spake
To Moses to deliver unto all
That song, because he knew they would let fall
The law, the prophets, and the history,
But keep the song still in their memory:

Such an opinion in due measure made
Me this great office boldly to invade,
Nor could incomprehensibleness deter
Me from thus trying to imprison her;
Which when I saw that a strict grave could do,
I saw not why verse might not do so too.
Verse hath a middle nature; heaven keeps souls,
The grave keeps bodies, verse the fame enrolls.

A *Funeral Elegy.*

'T is loss[1] to trust a tomb with such a guest,
Or to confine her in a marble chest;
Alas! what 's marble, jet, or porphyry,
Prized with the chrysolite of either eye,
Or with those pearls and rubies which she was?
Join the two Indies in one tomb, 't is glass;
And so is all to her materials,
Though every inch were ten Escurials;
Yet she 's demolished; can we keep her then
In works of hands or of the wits of men?
Can these memorials, rags of paper, give
Life to that name, by which name they must live?
Sickly, alas! short-lived, aborted[2] be
Those carcase verses whose soul is not she;
And can she, who no longer would be she
(Being such a tabernacle), stoop to be
In paper wrapped, or, when she would not lie
In such a[3] house, dwell in an elegy?

1 lost, 1633. 2 abortive. 3 an.

But 't is no matter; we may well allow
Verse to live so long as the world will now,
For her death wounded it.   The world contains
Princes for arms and counsellors for brains,
Lawyers for tongues, divines for hearts and more,
The rich for stomachs, and for backs the poor,
The officers for hands, merchants for feet
By which remote and distant countries meet;
But those fine spirits which do tune and set
This organ are those pieces which beget
Wonder and love; and these were she, and she
Being spent, the world must needs decrepit be:
For since Death will proceed to triumph still,
He can find nothing after her to kill,
Except the world itself, so great was she.
Thus brave and confident may Nature be
Death cannot give her such another blow,
Because she cannot such another show.
But must we say she 's dead? may 't not be said
That as a sundered clock is piecemeal laid,
Not to be lost, but by the maker's hand
Repolished, without error then to stand,
Or, as the Afric Niger stream enwombs
Itself into the earth, and after comes
(Having first made a natural bridge to pass
For many leagues) far greater than it was,
May 't not be said that her grave shall restore
Her greater, purer, firmer than before?
Heaven may say this, and joy in 't; but can we
Who live and lack her here this vantage see?

What is 't to us, alas! if there have been
An Angel made a Throne or Cherubin?
We lose by 't, and, as aged men are glad,
Being tasteless grown, to joy in joys they had,
So now the sick-starved world must feed upon
This joy, that we had her who now is gone.
Rejoice then, Nature and this World, that you,
Fearing the last fire's hastening to subdue
Your force and vigour, ere it were near gone,
Wisely bestowed and laid it all on one,
One whose clear body was so pure and thin,
Because it need disguise no thought within,
'T was but a through-light scarf her mind to enroll,
Or exhalation breathed out from her soul,
One whom all men, who durst no more, admired,
And whom, who'er had worth [1] enough, desired,
As, when a temple 's built, saints emulate
To which of them it shall be consecrate.
But, as when heaven looks on us with new eyes,
Those new stars every artist exercise;
What place they should assign to them they doubt,
Argue, and agree not, till those stars go out,
So the world studied whose this piece should be,
Till she can be no body's else, nor she:
But like a lamp of balsamum, desired
Rather t' adorn than last, she soon expired,
Clothed in her virgin-white integrity;
For marriage, though it doth not stain, doth dye.
To scape th' infirmities which wait upon
Woman, she went away before she was one,

1 worke, 1633.

And, the world's busy noise to overcome,
Took so much death as served for opium ;
For though she could not, nor could choose to die,
She 'th yielded to too long an ecstasy.
He which, not knowing her said[1] history,
Should come to read the book of destiny,
How fair and chaste, humble and high she'd been,
Much promised, much performed at not fifteen,
And measuring future things by things before,
Should turn the leaf to read, and read no more,
Would think that either destiny mistook,
Or that some leaves were torn out of the book ;
But 't is not so : Fate did but usher her
To years of reason's use, and then infer
Her destiny to herself, which liberty
She took but for thus much, thus much to die ;
Her modesty not suffering her to be
Fellow-commissioner with destiny,
She did no more but die ; if after her
Any shall live which dare true good prefer,
Every such person is her delegate
T' accomplish that which should have been her fate.
They shall make up that book, and shall have thanks
Of Fate and her for filling up their blanks.
For future virtuous deeds are legacies
Which from the gift of her example rise,
And 't is in heaven part of spiritual mirth
To see how well the good play her on earth.

[1] sad.

OF THE PROGRESS OF THE SOUL.

WHEREIN BY OCCASION OF THE RELIGIOUS DEATH OF MIS-
TRESS ELIZABETH DRURY, THE INCOMMODITIES OF THE
SOUL IN THIS LIFE AND HER EXALTATION IN THE NEXT
ARE CONTEMPLATED.

THE HARBINGER TO THE PROGRESS.[1]

Two souls move here, and mine (a third) must move
Paces of admiration and of love.
Thy soul (dear virgin) whose this tribute is,
Moved from this mortal sphere to lively bliss,
And yet moves still, and still aspires to see
The world's last day, thy glory's full degree,
Like as those stars, which thou o'erlookest far,
Are in their place and yet still movëd are :
No soul (whiles with the luggage of this clay
It cloggëd is) can follow thee half way,
Or see thy flight which doth our thoughts outgo
So fast that[2] now the lightning moves but slow.
But now thou art as high in heaven flown
As heaven 's from us, what soul besides thine own
Can tell thy joys, or say he can relate
Thy glorious journals in that blessed state ?
I envy thee, rich soul, I envy thee,
Although I cannot yet thy glory see :

---

1 This " Harbinger," according to Jonson, was Bishop Hall.
2 as.

And thou, great spirit, which her's followed hast
So fast, as none can follow thine so fast,
So far, as none can follow thine so far,
(And if this flesh did not the passage bar,
Hadst caught her) let me wonder at thy flight,
Which long agone hadst lost the vulgar sight,
And now mak'st proud the better eyes that they
Can see thee lessened in thine airy way ;
So while thou mak'st her soul by progress known,
Thou mak'st a noble progress of thine own,
From this world's carcase having mounted high
To that pure life of immortality ;
Since thine aspiring thoughts themselves so raise
That more may not beseem a creature's praise,
Yet still thou vow'st her more, and every year
Mak'st a new progress while thou wand'rest here,
Still upward mount, and let thy Maker's praise
Honour thy Laura and adorn thy lays :
And since thy Muse her head in heaven shrouds,
Oh, let her never stoop below the clouds !
And if those glorious sainted souls may know
Or what we do, or what we sing below,
Those acts, those songs shall still content them best,
Which praise those awful Powers that make them blest.

OF THE PROGRESS OF THE SOUL.

THE SECOND ANNIVERSARY.

NOTHING could make me sooner to confess
That this world had an everlastingness,
Than to consider that a year is run
Since both this lower world's and the sun's sun,
The lustre and the vigour of this All,
Did set, 't were blasphemy to say, did fall.
But, as a ship which hath struck sail doth run
By force of that force which before it won,
Or as sometimes in a beheaded man,
Though at those two red seas which freely ran,
One from the trunk, another from the head,
His soul be [1] sailed to her eternal bed,
His eyes will twinkle and his tongue will roll,
As though he beckoned and called back his soul,
He grasps his hands and he pulls up his feet,
And seems to reach and to step forth to meet
His soul, when all these motions which we saw,
Are but as ice which crackles at a thaw,
Or as a lute which in moist weather rings
Her knell alone by cracking of her strings ;
So struggles this dead world, now she is gone :
For there is motion in corruptïon.
As some days are at the creation named
Before the sun, the which framed days, was framed,

[1] he, 1633.

So after this sun's set some show appears,
And orderly vicissitude of years;
Yet a new deluge, and of Lethe flood,
Hath drowned us all; all have forgot all good,
Forgetting her, the main reserve of all;
Yet in this deluge gross and general
Thou seest me strive for life; my life shall be
To be hereafter praised for praising thee,
Immortal maid, who though thou would'st refuse
The name of mother, be unto my Muse
A father, since her chaste ambition is
Yearly to bring forth such a child as this.
These hymns may work on future wits and so
May great grand-children of thy praises grow,
And so, though not revive, embalm and spice
The world which else would putrefy with vice.
For thus man may extend thy progeny
Until man do but vanish, and not die.
These hymns thy issue may increase so long
As till God's great *Venite* change the song.
Thirst for that time, O my insatiate soul,
And serve thy thirst with God's safe-sealing bowl.
Be thirsty still and drink still till thou go
To th' only health; to be hydroptic so,
Forget this rotten world, and unto thee
Let thine own times as an old story be;
Be not concerned; study not why nor[1] when,
Do not so much as not believe a man;

A just dises-
timation of
this world.

1 or, 1669.

For though to err be worst, to try truths forth
Is far more business than this world is worth.
The world is but a carcase ; thou art fed
By it but as a worm that carcase bred ;
And why should'st thou, poor worm, consider more
When this world will grow better than before,
Than those thy fellow-worms do think upon
That carcase's last resurrectiön ?
Forget this world, and scarce think of it so
As of old clothes cast off a year ago :
To be thus stupid is alacrity ;
Men thus lethargic have best memory.
Look upward, that 's towards her whose happy state
We now lament not, but congratulate.
She, to whom all this world was but a stage
Where all sat hearkening how her youthful age
Should be employed, because in all she did
Some figure of the golden times was hid,
Who could not lack whate'er this world could give,
Because she was the form that made it live,
Nor could complain that this world was unfit
To be stayed in then when she was in it,
She, that first tried indifferent desires
By virtue, and virtue by religious fires,
She, to whose person paradise adhered,
As Courts to princes, she, whose eyes ensphered
Star-light enough t' have made the south control
(Had she been there) the starful northern pole,
She, she is gone ; she is gone: when thou knowest this,
What fragmentary rubbish this world is

II.—7.

Thou knowest, and that it is not worth a thought;
He honours it too much that thinks it nought.

Contempla-
tion of our
state in our
death-bed.

Think then, my soul, that Death is but a groom
Which brings a taper to the outward room,
Whence thou spiest first a little glimmering light,
And after brings it nearer to thy sight;
For such approaches doth heaven make in death :
Think thyself labouring now with broken breath,
And think those broken and soft notes to be
Division, and thy happiest harmony;
Think thee laid on thy death-bed, loose and slack,
And think that, but unbinding of a pack
To take one precious thing, thy soul, from thence;
Think thyself parched [1] with fever's violence;
Anger thine ague more by calling it
Thy physic; chide the slackness of the fit;
Think that thou hear'st thy knell, and think no more
But that, as bells called thee to church before,
So this to the triumphant church calls thee;
Think Satan's sergeants round about thee be,
And think that but for legacies they thrust; [2]
Give one thy pride, to another give thy lust;
Give them those sins which they gave thee before,
And trust th' immaculate blood to wash thy score;
Think thy friends weeping round, and think that they
Weep but because they go not yet thy way;
Think that they close thine eyes, and think in this,
That they confess much in the world amiss

1 patched, 1633, '35.   2 trust, 1669.

Who dare not trust a dead man's eye with that
Which they from God and angels cover not;
Think that they shroud thee up, and think from thence,
They re-invest thee in white innocence;
Think that thy body rots, and (if so low,
Thy soul exalted so, thy thoughts can go,)
Think thee a prince, who of themselves create
Worms which insensibly devour their state;
Think that they bury thee, and think that rite
Lays thee to sleep but a Saint Lucy's night.
Think these things cheerfully, and if thou be
Drowsy or slack, remember then that she,
She, whose complexion was so even made
That which of her ingredients should invade
The other three, no fear, no art could guess,
So far were all removed from more or less,
But as in mithridate, or just perfumes,
Where all good things being met, no one presumes
To govern, or to triumph on the rest,
Only because all were, no part was, best;
And as, though all do know that quantities
Are made of lines, and lines from points arise,
None can these lines or quantities unjoint,
And say, this is a line, or this a point,
So, though the elements and humours were
In her, one could not say, this governs there,
Whose even constitution might have won
Any disease to venture on the sun
Rather than her, and make a spirit fear
That he to disuniting subject were;

To whose proportions if we would compare
Cubes, they 're unstable ; circles, angular ;
·She, who was such a chain as fate employs
To bring mankind all fortunes it enjoys,
So fast, so even wrought, as one would think
No accident could threaten any link ;
She, she embraced a sickness, gave it meat,
The purest blood and breath that e'er it eat;
And hath taught us that, though a good man hath
Title to heaven, and plead it by his faith,
And though he may pretend a conquest, since
Heaven was content to suffer violence,
Yea, though he plead a long possession too,
(For they 're in heaven on earth, who heaven's works do)
Though he had right and power and place before,
Yet Death must usher and unlock the door.
Think further on thyself, my soul, and think
How thou at first wast made but in a sink ;
Think, that it argued some infirmity,
That those two souls, which then thou found'st in me,
Thou fed'st upon, and drew'st into thee both
My second soul of sense, and first of growth ;
Think but how poor thou wast, how óbnoxious,
Whom a small lump of flesh could poison thus :
This curded milk, this poor unlittered whelp,
My body, could, beyond escape or help,
Infect thee with original sin, and thou
Could'st neither then refuse, nor leave it now;
Think that no stubborn sullen anchorit
Which, fixed to a pillar or a grave, doth sit

Bedded and bathed in all his ordures, dwells
So foully as our souls in their first-built cells;
Think in how poor a prison thou didst[1] lie,
After, enabled but to suck and cry;
Think, when 't was grown to most, 't was a poor inn,
A province packed up in two yards of skin,
And that usurped, or threatened with a rage
Of sicknesses, or their true mother, age;
But think that death hath now enfranchised thee,
Thou hast thy expansion now, and liberty;
Think that a rusty piece discharged is flown
In pieces, and the bullet is his own
And freely flies; this to thy soul allow;
Think thy shell broke, think thy soul hatched but now;
And think this slow-paced soul which late did cleave
To a body, and went but by the body's leave
Twenty, perchance, or thirty mile a day,
Despatches in a minute all the way
Twixt heaven and earth; she stays not in the air
To look what meteors there themselves prepare;
She carries no desire to know, nor sense,
Whether th' air's middle region be intense;
For th' element of fire, she doth not know
Whether she passed by such a place or no;
She baits not at the moon, nor cares to try
Whether in that new world men live and die;
Venus retards her not to inquire how she
Can (being one star) Hesper and Vesper be;
He that charmed Argus' eyes, sweet Mercury,
Works not on her who now is grown all eye,

*Her liberty
by death.*

1 dost, 1669.

Who, if she meet the body of the sun,
Goes through, not staying till his course be run,
Who finds in Mars his camp no corps of guard.
Nor is by Jove, nor by his father, barred,
But ere she can consider how she went,
At once is at and through the firmament.
And, as these stars were but so many beads
Strung on one string, speed undistinguished leads
Her through those spheres, as through the[1] beads a string
Whose quick succession makes it still one thing:
As doth the pith, which, lest our bodies slack,
Strings fast the little bones of neck and back,
So by the soul doth death string heaven and earth;
For when our soul enjoys this her[2] third birth,
(Creation gave her one, a second, Grace)
Heaven is as near[3] and present to her face
As colours are and objects in a room,
Where darkness was before, when tapers come.
This must, my soul, thy long-short progress be
T' advance these thoughts; remember then that she,
She, whose fair body no such prison was
But that a soul might well be pleased to pass
An age in her; she, whose rich beauty lent
Mintage to other beauties, for they went
But for so much as they were like to her;
She, in whose body (if we dare prefer
This low world to so high a mark as she,)
The western treasure, eastern spicery,
Europe and Afric and the unknown rest
Were easily found, or what in them was best;

1 those, 1669. 2 enjoys her, 1649, '54, '69. 3 is near, 1669.

And when we 've made this large discovery
Of all, in her some one part then will be
Twenty such parts, whose plenty and riches is
Enough to make [1] twenty such worlds as this ;
She, whom had they known, who did first betroth
The tutelar angels, and assigned one both
To nations, cities, and to companies,
To functions, offices, and dignities,
And to each several man, to him, and him,
They would have given her one for every limb ;
She, of whose soul if we may say 't was gold,
Her body was th' electrum, and did hold
Many degrees of that ; we understood
Her by her sight ; her pure and eloquent blood
Spoke in her cheeks, and so distinctly wrought
That one might almost say her body thought ;
She, she thus richly and largely housed, is gone,
And chides us slow-paced snails who crawl upon
Our prison's prison, earth, nor think us well
Longer than whilst we bear our brittle shell.
But 't were but little to have changed our room,
If, as we were in this our living tomb
Oppressed with ignorance, we still were so.
Poor soul, in this thy flesh what dost thou know ?
Thou know'st thyself so little, as thou know'st not
How thou didst die nor how thou wast begot ;
Thou neither know'st how thou at first cam'st in
Nor how thou took'st the poison of man's sin ;
Nor dost thou, (though thou know'st that thou art so,)
By what way thou art made immortal, know.

1 wake, 1635, '39.

Thou art too narrow, wretch, to comprehend
Even thyself, yea, though thou would'st but bend
To know thy body.   Have not all souls thought
For many ages that our body is wrought
Of air and fire and other elements?
And now they think of new ingredients;
And one soul thinks one, and another way
Another thinks, and 't is an even lay.
Know'st thou but how the stone doth enter in
The bladder's cave and never break the skin?
Know'st thou how blood, which to the heart doth flow,
Doth from one ventricle to th' other go?
And for the putrid stuff which thou dost spit,
Know'st thou how thy lungs have attracted it?
There are no passages; so that there is
(For ought thou know'st) piercing of substances.
And of those many opinions which men raise
Of nails and hairs, dost thou know which to praise?
What hope have we to know ourselves, when we
Know not the least things which for our use be?
We see in authors too stiff to recant,
A hundred controversies of an ant;
And yet one watches, starves, freezes, and sweats,
To know but catechisms and alphabets
Of unconcerning things, matters of fact;
How others on our stage their parts did act,
What Cæsar did, yea, and what Cicero said;
Why grass is green, or why our blood is red,
Are mysteries which none have reached unto;
In this low form, poor soul, what wilt thou do?

When wilt thou shake off this pedántery [1]
Of being taught by sense and fantasy?
Thou look'st through spectacles ; small things seem great
Below ; but up unto the watch-tower get
And see all things despoiled of fallacies :
Thou shalt not peep through lattices of eyes,
Nor hear through labyrinths of ears, nor learn
By circuit or collections to discern ;
In heaven thou straight know'st all concerning it,
And what concerns it not shalt straight forget.
There thou (but in no other school) may'st be
Perchance as learnëd and as full as she ;
She, who all libraries had throughly read
At home in her own thoughts, and practisëd
So much good as would make as many more ;
She, whose example they must all implore,
Who would or do or think well, and confess
That all the virtuous actions they express,
Are but a new and worse editiön
Of her some one thought, or one actiön ;
She who in th' art of knowing heaven was grown
Here upon earth to such perfectiön
That she hath, ever since to heaven she came,
In a far fairer print [2] but read the same ;
She, she not satisfied with all this weight,
(For so much knowledge as would overfreight
Another, did but ballast her) is gone
As well t' enjoy, as get, perfectiön,

1 pedantry, 1649, '54, '69.   2 point, 1633.

And calls us after her in that she took
(Taking herself) our best and worthiest book.

*Of our com-
pany in this
life and in
the next.*
Return not, my soul, from this ecstasy
And meditation of what thou shalt be,
To earthly thoughts, till it to thee appear,
With whom thy conversation must be there.
With whom wilt thou converse? what station
Canst thou choose out free from infection,
That will not give thee theirs, nor drink-in thine?
Shalt thou not find a spongy slack divine
Drink and suck in th' instructions of great men,
And for the word of God vent them agen?
Are there not some Courts (and then no things be
So like as Courts) which in this let us see
That wits and tongues of libellers are weak,
Because they do more ill than these can speak?
The poison 's gone through all; poisons affect
Chiefly the chiefest parts, but some effect
In nails and hairs, yea, excrements, will show,
So lies the poison of sin in the most low.
Up, up, my drowsy soul, where thy new ear
Shall in the angels' songs no discord hear;
Where thou shalt see the blessed Mother-maid
Joy in not being that which men have said;
Where she is exalted more for being good
Than for her interest of motherhood;
Up to those Patriarchs which did longer sit
Expecting Christ than they have enjoyed him yet;
Up to those Prophets which now gladly see
Their prophesies grown to be history;

Up to th' Apostles who did bravely run
All the sun's course with more light than the sun;
Up to those Martyrs who did calmly bleed
Oil to the Apostle's lamps, dew to their seed;
Up to those Virgins who thought that almost
They made joint-tenants with the Holy Ghost,
If they to any should his temple give;
Up, up, for in that squadron there doth live
She who hath carried thither new degrees
(As to their number) to their dignities;
She who, being to herself a state, enjoyed
All royalties which any state employed;
For she made wars and triumphed; reason still
Did not o'erthrow, but rectify her will;
And she made peace; for no peace is like this,
That beauty and chastity together kiss;
She did high justice; for she crucified
Every first motion of rebellious [1] pride;
And she gave pardons, and was liberal,
For, only herself except, she pardoned all;
She coined in this, that her impression gave
To all our actions all the worth they have;
She gave protections; the thoughts of her breast
Satan's rude officers could ne'er arrest.
As these prerogatives, being met in one,
Made her a sovereign state, religiön
Made her a church; and these two made her all.
She who was all this All, and could not fall
To worse by company, (for she was still
More antidote than all the world was ill,)

[1] rebellion's.

She, she doth leave it, and by death survive
All this in heaven; whither who doth not strive
The more because she 's there, he doth not know
That accidental joys in heaven do grow.
But pause, my soul, and study, ere thou fall
On accidental joys, th' essentiäl;
Still before accessóries do abide
A trial, must the principal be tried;
Of essential And what essential joy canst thou expect
joy in this Here upon earth? what permanent effect
life and in
the next. Of transitory causes?   Dost thou love
Beauty? (and beauty worthiest is to move,)
Poor cozened cozener, *that* she and *that* thou
Which did begin to love, are neither now;
You are both fluid, changed since yesterday;
Next day repairs (but ill) last day's decay,
Nor are (although the river keep the name)
Yesterday's waters and to-day's the same;
So flows her face and thine eyes; neither now
That saint nor pilgrim which your loving vow
Concerned, remains; but whilst you think you be
Constant, you are hourly in inconstancy.
Honour may have pretence unto our love,
Because that God did live so long above
Without this honour, and then loved it so
That he at last made creatures to bestow
Honour on him, not that he needed it,
But that to his hands man might grow more fit.
But since all honours from inferiors flow,
(For they do give it, princes do but show

Whom they would have so honoured,) and that this
On such opinions and capacities
Is built as rise and fall to more and less,
Alas! 't is but a casual happiness.
Hath ever any man to himself assigned
This or that happiness to arrest his mind,
But that another man, which takes a worse,
Thinks him a fool for having ta'en that course?
They who did labour Babel's tower to erect
Might have considered that for that effect
All this whole solid earth could not allow
Nor furnish forth materials enow,[1]
And that his centre, to raise such a place,
Was far too little to have been the base;
No more affords this world foundatiön
To erect true joy, were all the means in one.
But as the heathen made them several gods
Of all God's benefits and all his rods,
(For as the wine and corn and onions are
Gods unto them, so agues be, and war,)
And as by changing that whole precious gold
To such small copper coins, they lost the old,
And lost their only God, who ever must
Be sought alone, and not in such a thrust,
So much mankind true happiness mistakes;
No joy enjoys that man that many makes.
Then, soul, to thy first pitch work up again;
Know that all lines which circles do contain,
For once that they the centre touch, do touch
Twice the circumference, and be thou such;

1 enough, 1633.

Double on heaven thy thoughts; on earth employed,
All will not serve; only who have enjoyed
The sight of God in fulness, can think it,
For it is both the object and the wit;
This is essential joy, where neither he
Can suffer diminutiön, nor we;
'T is such a full and such a filling good,
Had th' angels once looked on him, they had stood.
To fill the place of one of them, or more,
She, whom we celebrate, is gone before;
She, who had here so much essential joy
As no chance could distract, much less destroy;
Who with God's presence was acquainted so
(Hearing, and speaking to him) as to know
His face in any natural stone or tree
Better than when in images they be;
Who kept by diligent devotiön
God's image in such reparatiön
Within her heart, that what decay was grown,
Was her first parents' fault and not her own;
Who, being solicited to any act,
Still heard God pleading his safe precontract;
Who by a faithful confidence was here
Betrothed to God, and now is married there;
Whose twilights were more clear than our mid-day;
Who dreamt devoutlier than most use to pray;
Who, being here filled with grace, yet strove to be
Both where more grace and more capacity
At once is given; she to heaven is gone,
Who made this world in some proportiön

A heaven, and here became unto us all
Joy (as our joys admit) essentiäl.
But could this low world joys essential touch,
Heaven's accidental joys would pass them much;
How poor and lame must then our casual be?

Of accidental joys in both places.

If thy prince will his subjects to call thee
My Lord, and this do swell thee, thou art than,
By being greater, grown to be less man.
When no physician of redress can speak,
A joyful casual violence may break
A dangerous apostem in thy breast,
And, whilst thou joyest in this, the dangerous rest,
The bag, may rise up, and so strangle thee.
What e'er was casual, may ever be:
What should the nature change? or make the same
Certain, which was but casual when it came?
All casual joy doth loud and plainly say,
Only by coming, that it can away.
Only in heaven joy's strength is never spent
And accidental things are permanent.
Joy of a soul's arrival ne'er decays,
For that soul ever joys and ever stays;
Joy that their last great consummatiön
Approaches in the resurrectiön,
When earthly bodies more celestiäl
Shall be than angels were, for they could fall,
This kind of joy doth every day admit
Degrees of growth, but none of losing it.
In this fresh joy, 't is no small part that she,
She, in whose goodness he that names degree

Doth injure her, ('t is loss to be called best,
There where the stuff is not such as the rest) ;
She who left such a body as even she
Only in heaven could learn how it can be
Made better, for she rather was two souls,
Or like to full on-both-sides-written rolls
Where eyes might read upon the outward skin
As strong recórds for God, as minds within ;
She who, by making full perfection grow,
Pieces a circle and still keeps it so,
Longed for and longing for it, to heaven is gone,
Where she receives and gives additiön.
Here, in a place where misdevotion frames

Conclusion. A thousand prayers to saints whose very names
The ancient church knew not, heaven knows not yet,
And where what laws of poetry admit,
Laws of religion have at least the same,
Immortal Maid, I might invoke thy name.
Could any saint provoke that appetite,
Thou here should'st make me a French convertite ;
But thou would'st not ; nor would'st thou be content
To take this for my second year's true rent,
Did this coin bear any other stamp than his
That gave thee power to do, me, to say this :
Since his will is that to posterity
Thou should'st for life and death a pattern be,
And that the world should notice have of this,
The purpose and th' authority is his ;
Thou art the proclamation ; and I am
The trumpet at whose voice the people came.

EPICEDES AND OBSEQUIES UPON THE DEATHS OF SUNDRY PERSONAGES.[1]

ELEGY ON PRINCE HENRY.[2]

Look to me, faith, and look to my faith, God;
For both my centres feel this period.
Of weight one centre, one of greatness is;
And reason is that centre, faith is this;
For into our reason flow, and there do end,
All that this natural world doth comprehend,
Quotidian things and equidistant hence
Shut in for man in one circumference;
But for th' enormous greatnesses which are
So disproportioned and so angular
As is God's essence, place, and providence,
Where, how, when, what souls do, departed hence,
These things (eccentric else) on faith do strike,
Yet neither all, nor upon all, alike.
For reason, put to her best extensïon,
Almost meets faith and makes both centres one;
And nothing ever came so near to this
As contemplation of that Prince we miss;
For all that Faith might credit mankind could,
Reason still seconded that this prince would.

1 This general title is not given in the edition of 1633.
2 An elegy on the untimely death of the incomparable Prince Henry, 1669.
II.—8.

If then least moving of the centre make
More than if whole hell belched the world to shake,
What must this do, centres distracted so
That we see not what to believe or know?
Was it not well believed till now, that he
Whose reputation was an ecstasy
On neighbour states, which knew not why to wake
Till he discovered what ways he would take;
For whom what princes angled, when they tried,
Met a torpedo and were stupefied;
And others studies[1] how he would be bent,
Was his great father's greatest instrument
And activest spirit to convey and tie
This soul of peace through[2] Christianity?
Was it not well believed that he would make
This general peace th' eternal overtake,
And that his times might have stretched out so far
As to touch those of which they emblems are?
For to confirm this just belief that now
The last days came, we saw heaven did allow
That, but from his aspéct and exercise,
In peaceful times rumors of wars did[3] rise.
But now this faith is heresy: we must
Still stay and vex our great grandmother, Dust.
Oh, is God prodigal? hath he spent his store
Of plagues on us, and only now, when more
Would ease us much, doth he grudge misery,
And will not let 's enjoy our curse, to die?

1 studied (?).   2 to.   3 should.

As, for the earth thrown lowest down of all,
'T were an ambition to desire to fall,
So God, in our desire to die, doth know
Our plot for ease in being wretched so ;
Therefore we live, though such a life we have
As but so many mandrakes on his grave.
What had his growth and generation done,
When what we are, his putrefaction
Sustains in us, earth, which griefs animate ?
Nor hath our world now other soul than that.
And could grief get so high as heaven, that choir,
Forgetting this their new joy, would desire
(With grief to see him) he had stayed below
To rectify our errors they foreknow.
Is th' other centre, reason, faster then ?
Where should we look for that, now we 're not men ?
For if our reason be our connection
Of causes, now to us there can be none.
For as, if all the substances were spent,
'T were madness to inquire of accident,
So is 't to [1] look for reason, he being gone,
The only subject reason wrought upon.
If Fate have such a chain, whose divers links
Industrious man discerneth, as he thinks,
When miracle doth come, and so steal in
A new link, man knows not where to begin ;
At a much deader fault must reason be,
Death having broke off such a link as he.

1 So is to, 1669.

But now, for us with busy proof to come
That we 've no reason, would prove we had some ;
So would just lamentations : therefore we
May safelier say that we are dead, than he.
So, if our griefs we do not well declare,
We 've double excuse ; he 's not dead, and we are.[1]
Yet I would not die yet;[2] for though I be
Too narrow to think him as he is he,
(Our soul's best baiting and mid-period
In her long journey of considering God)
Yet, (no dishonour) I can reach him thus,
As he embraced the fires of love with us.
Oh may I (since I live) but see or hear
That she-intelligence which moved this sphere,
I pardon fate my life; who e'er thou be,
Which hast the noble conscience, thou art she,
I conjure thee by all the charms he spoke,
By th' oaths which only you two never broke,
By all the souls ye sighed, that if you see
These lines, you wish I knew your history;
So much as you two mutual heavens were here,
I were an angel, singing what you were.

1 We have double excuse, he 's not dead, we are, 1669.
2 Yet would not I die yet, *ibid.*

OBSEQUIES TO THE LORD HARRINGTON,

BROTHER [1] TO THE COUNTESS OF BEDFORD.

To the Countess of Bedford.

MADAM,

I HAVE learned by those laws, wherein I am [2] a little conversant, that he which bestows any cost upon the dead, obliges him which is dead, but not the [3] heir; I do not therefore send this paper to your Ladyship that you should thank me for it, or think that I thank you in it; your favours and benefits to me are so much above my merits, that they are even above my gratitude, if that were to be judged by words, which must express it. But, Madam, since your noble brother's fortune being yours, the evidences also concerning it are yours; so his virtue [4] being yours, the evidences concerning it [5] belong also to you, of which by your acceptance this may be one piece; in which quality I humbly present it, and as a testimony how entirely your family possesseth

Your Ladyship's
Most humble and thankful servant,
JOHN DONNE.

FAIR soul, which wast not only as all souls be,
Then when thou wast infusëd, harmony,
But did'st continue so, and now dost bear
A part in God's great organ, this whole sphere ;

---

1 to the Lord Harrington's brother, 1633, '39, '40, '54; on the Lord Harrington, etc., 1669. 2 I am little conversant, 1669. 3 his, *ibid.* 4 virtues. 5 that.

II.—8*.

If, looking up to God, or down to us,
Thou find that any way is pervious
'Twixt heaven and earth, and that man's [1] actions do
Come to your knowledge and affections too,
See, and with joy, me to that good degree
Of goodness grown, that I can study thee,
And by these meditatiöns refined,
Can unapparel and enlarge my mind,
And so can make by this soft ecstasy,
This place a map of heaven, myself of thee.
Thou seest me here at midnight now, all rest;
Time's dead-low water, when all minds devest
To-morrow's business; when the labourers have
Such rest in bed, that their last church-yard grave,
Subject to change, will scarce be a type of this;
Now when the client, whose last hearing is
To-morrow, sleeps; when the condemnëd man,
(Who, when he opes his eyes, must shut them than
Again by death,) although sad watch he keep,
Doth practise dying by a little sleep;
Thou at this midnight seest me, and as soon
As that sun rises to me, midnight's noon,
All the world grows transparent, and I see
Through all, both Church and State, in seeing thee;
And I discern by favour of this light
Myself the hardest [2] object of the sight.
God is the glass; as thou, when thou dost see
Him who sees all, seest all concerning thee,
So, yet unglorified, I comprehend
All in these mirrors of thy ways and end.

[1] men's.   [2] hardyest, 1669.

Though God be our true glass, through which we see
All, since the being of all things is he,
Yet are the trunks which do to us derive
Things in proportion fit by perspective,
Deeds of good men : for by their being here,
Virtues, indeed remote, seem to be near.
But where can I affirm or where arrest
My thoughts on his deeds? which shall I call best?
For fluid virtue cannot be looked on,
Nor can endure a contemplation.
As bodies change, and as I do not wear
Those spirits, humours, blood, I did last year,
And as, if on a stream I fix mine eye,
That drop which I looked on is presently
Pushed with more waters from my sight and gone,
So in this sea of virtues can no one
Be insisted on; virtues as rivers pass,
Yet still remains that virtuous man there was.
And as, if man feeds[1] on man's flesh and so
Part of his body to another owe,
Yet at the last two perfect bodies rise,
Because God knows where every atom lies,
So, if one knowledge were made of all those,
Who knew his minutes well, he might dispose
His virtues into names and ranks; but I
Should injure Nature, Virtue, and Destiny,
Should I divide and discontinue so
Virtue which did in one entireness grow.
For as he that would[2] say, spirits are framed
Of all the purest parts that can be named,

1 feed. 2 should.

Honours not spirits half so much as he
Which says they have no parts, but simple be,
So is 't of virtue; for a point and one
Are much entirer than a milliön.
And had Fate meant to have[1] his virtues told,
It would have let him live to have been old;
So then that virtue in season, and then this,
We might have seen, and said that now he is
Witty, now wise, now temperate, now just.
In good short lives virtues are fain to thrust,
And, to be sure betimes to get a place,
When they would exercise, lack[2] time and space,
So was it in this person, forced to be,
For lack of time, his own epitome,
So to exhibit in few years as much
As all the long-breathed chronicles can touch.
As when an angel down from heaven doth fly,
Our quick thought cannot keep him company;
We cannot think, now he is at the sun,
Now through the moon, now he through th'[3] air
        doth run,
Yet when he 's come, we know he did repair
To all 'twixt heaven and earth, sun, moon, and air;
And as this angel in an instant knows,
And yet we know this sudden knowledge grows
By quick amassing several forms of things,
Which he successively to order brings,
When they, whose slow-paced lame thoughts cannot go
So fast as he, think that he doth not so,

1 t' have had. 2 last, 1669. 3 now through th' air, 1669.

(Just as a perfect reader doth not dwell
On every syllable, nor stay to spell,
Yet without doubt he doth distinctly see
And lay together every A and B,)
So in short-lived good men is not understood
Each several virtue, but the compound good;
For they all virtue's paths in that pace tread,
As angels go and know, and as men read.
Oh, why should then these men, these lumps of balm,
Sent hither the world's tempest to becalm,
Before by deeds they are diffused and spread,
And so make us alive, themselves be dead?
O soul! O circle! why so quickly be
Thy ends, thy birth and death, closed up in thee?
Since one foot of thy compass still was placed
In heaven, the other might securely have paced
In the most large extent through every path
Which the whole world, or man, the abridgment, hath.
Thou know'st that though the tropic circles have
(Yea, and those small ones which the poles engrave)
All the same roundness, evenness, and all
The endlessness of the equinoctiäl,
Yet when we come to measure distances,
How here, how there the sun affected is,
When he doth faintly work, and when prevail,
Only great circles then can be our scale ;
So, though thy circle to thyself express
All, tending to thy endless happiness,
And we, by our good use of it, may try
Both how to live well young and how to die,

Yet, since we must be old, and age endures
His torrid zone at court, and calentures
Of hot ambitions,[1] irreligion's ice,
Zeal's agues, and hydroptic avarice,
(Infirmities which need the scale of truth,
As well as lust and ignorance of youth)
Why didst thou not for these give medicines too,
And by thy doing tell[2] us what to do?
Though, as small pocket-clocks, whose every wheel
Doth each mis-motion and distemper feel,
Whose hands get[3] shaking palsies, and whose string,
His sinews, slackens, and whose soul, the spring,
Expires or languishes, whose pulse, the fly,[4]
Either beats not, or beats unevenly,
Whose voice, the bell, doth rattle or grow dumb,
Or idle, as men which to their last hours[5] come,
If these clocks be not wound, or be wound still,
Or be not set, or set at every will,
So youth is easiest to destructiön,
If then we follow all, or follow none;
Yet as in great clocks which in steeples chime,
Placed to inform whole towns to employ their time,
An error doth more harm, being general,
When small clocks' faults only on the wearer fall,
So work the faults of age, on which the eye
Of children, servants, or the state rely;
Why would'st not thou, then, which hadst such a soul,
A clock so true as might the sun control,

---

1 ambition, 1669.   2 set, 1635, '39, '49, '54.   3 gets, 1669.   4 flee.
5 hour, 1669.

And daily hadst from him who gave it thee
Instructions such as it could never be
Disordered, stay here as a general
And great sun-dial to have set us all?
Oh why would'st thou be any[1] instrument
To this unnatural course? or why consent
To this, not miracle, but prodigy,
That when the ebbs longer than flowings be,
Virtue, whose flood did with thy youth begin,
Should so much faster ebb out than flow in?
Though her flood was[2] blown in by thy first breath,
All is at once sunk in the whirlpool, death;
Which word I would not name, but that I see
Death, else a desert, grown a court by thee.
Now I am sure that if a man would have
Good company, his entry is a grave.
Methinks all cities now but ant-hills be,
Where when the several labourers I see
For children, house, provision, taking pain,
They 're all but ants, carrying eggs, straw, and grain:
And church-yards are our cities unto which
The most repair that are in goodness rich;
There is the best concourse and confluence,
There are the holy suburbs, and from thence
Begins God's city, New Jerusalem,
Which doth extend her utmost gates to them:
At that gate then, triumphant soul, dost thou
Begin thy triumph. But since laws allow

1 wouldest thou be an, 1639, '49, '54, '69.   2 were.

That at the triumph-day the people may,
All that they will 'gainst the triumpher say,
Let me here use that freedom and express
My grief, though not to make thy triumph less.
By law to triumphs none admitted be,
Till they, as magistrates, get victory;
Though, then, to thy force all youth's foes did yield,
Yet, till fit time had brought thee to that field
To which thy rank in this state destined thee,
That there thy counsels might get victory,
And so in that capacity remove
All jealousies 'twixt prince and subject's love,
Thou could'st no title to this triumph have,
Thou didst intrude on death, usurpst[1] a grave.
Then,[2] (though victoriously) thou hadst fought as yet
But with thine own affections, with the heat
Of youth's desires and colds of ignorance,
But till thou should'st successfully advance
Thine arms 'gainst foreign enemies, which are
Both envy and acclamation[3] popular,
(For both these engines equally defeat,
Though by a divers mine, those which are great,)
Till then thy war was but a civil war,
For which to triumph none admitted are;
No more are they, who, though with good success,
In a defensive war their power express;
Before men triumph, the dominiön
Must be enlarged, and not preserved alone;

---

1 usurp. 2 That, 1633. 3 acclamations, 1669.

Why should'st thou, then, whose battles were to win
Thyself from those straits nature put thee in,
And to deliver up to God that state,
Of which he gave thee the vicariate,
(Which is thy soul and body) as entire
As he who takes endeavours [1] doth require,
But didst not stay t' enlarge his kingdom too,
By making others, what thou didst, to do;
Why should'st thou triumph now, when heaven no more
Hath got, by getting thee, than it had before?
For heaven and thou, even when thou livedst here,
Of one another in possession were.
But this from triumph most disables thee,
That that place which is conquerëd must be
Left safe from present war and likely doubt
Of imminent commotions to break out;
And hath he left us so? or can it be
His territory was no more than he?
No, we were all his charge; the diocis
Of every exemplar man the whole world is;
And he was joinëd in commissiön
With tutelar angels sent to every one.
But, though this freedom to upbraid and chide
Him who triümphed were lawful, it was tied
With this, that it might never reference have
Unto the senate who this triumph gave;
Men might at Pompey jest, but they might not
At that authority by which he got

1 indentours, 1669.

Leave to triúmph before by age he might ;
So though, triumphant soul, I dare to write,
Moved with a reverential anger, thus,
That thou so early would'st abandon us,
Yet I am far from daring to dispute
With that great sovereignty whose absolute
Prerogative hath thus dispensed with thee
'Gainst nature's laws, which just impugners be
Of early triumphs, and I (though with pain)
Lessen our loss, to magnify thy gain
Of triumph, when I say it was more fit
That all men should lack thee, than thou lack it.
Though, then, in our time[1] be not sufferëd
That testimony of love unto the dead,
To die with them and in their graves be hid,
As Saxon wives and French soldarii did,
· And though in no degree I can express
Grief in great Alexander's great excess,
Who at his friend's death made whole towns devest
Their walls and bulwarks which became them best,
Do not, fair soul, this sacrifice refuse,
That in thy grave I do inter my Muse,
Who[2] by my grief, great as thy worth, being cast
Behindhand, yet hath spoke, and spoke her last.

1 times, 1669. 2 Which.

AN ELEGY ON THE LADY MARKHAM.

MAN is the world and death th' ocean
To which God gives the lower parts of man.
This sea environs all, and though as yet
God hath set marks and bounds 'twixt us and it,
Yet doth it roar and gnaw and still pretend,
And breaks [1] our bank whene'er it takes a friend :
Then our land-waters (tears of passion) vent ;
Our waters then, above our firmament,
(Tears which our soul doth for her sins let fall,)
Take all a brackish taste and funeral,
And even those tears which should wash sin are sin;
We, after God's Noah, drown the world again.[2]
Nothing but man, of all envenomed things,
Doth work upon itself with inborn stings.
Tears are false spectacles; we cannot see
Through passion's mist what we are, or what she.
In her this sea of death hath made no breach,
But, as the tide doth wash the slimy beach
And leaves embroidered works upon the sand,
So is her flesh refined by death's cold hand.
As men of China, after an age's stay,
Do take up porcelain where they buried clay,
So at this grave, her limbec (which refines
The diamonds, rubies, sapphires, pearls, and mines

1 To break, 1669. 2 We, after God, new drown our world again, *ibid.*

Of which this flesh was,) her soul shall inspire
Flesh of such stuff as God, when his last fire
Annuls this world, to recompense it, shall
Make and name then [1] th' elixir of this All.
They say the sea, when it gains, loseth too ;
If carnal Death (the younger brother) do
Usurp the body, our soul, which subject is
To th' elder Death by sin, is freed by this;
They perish both, when they attempt the just;
For graves our trophies are and both Deaths' dust.
So, unobnoxious now, she hath buried both ;
For none to death sins that to sin is loth,
Nor do they die which are not loth to die ;
So hath she this and that virginity.
Grace was in her extremely diligent,
That kept her from sin, yet made her repent.
Of what small spots pure white complains ! Alas,
How little poison cracks a crystal glass !
She sinned but just enough to let us see
That God's word must be true, All sinners be.
So much did zeal her conscience rarefy, [2]
That extreme truth lacked little of a lie,
Making omissions acts, laying the touch
Of sin on things that sometimes [3] may be such.
As Moses' cherubins, whose natures do
Surpass all speed, by him are wingèd too, [4]
So would her soul, already in heaven, seem then
To climb by tears, the common stairs of men.

1 them, 1669. 2 This and the preceding verse are not in the edition
of 1633. 3 sometime. 4 to, 1635, '39, '49, '54.

How fit she was for God, I am content
To speak that Death his vain haste may repent :
How fit for us, how even and how sweet,
How good in all her titles, and how meet
To have reformed this forward heresy,
That woman [1] can no parts of friendship be,
How moral, how divine, shall not be told,
Lest they that hear her virtues think [2] her old,
And lest we take Death's part and make him glad
Of such a prey, and to his triumph add.

ELEGY ON MISTRESS BOULSTRED.

DEATH, I recant, and say unsaid by me
Whate'er hath slipped that might diminish thee :
Spiritual treason, atheism 't is, to say
That any can thy summons disobey.
Th' earth's face is but thy table; there are set
Plants, cattle, men, dishes [3] for Death to eat.
In a rude hunger now he millions draws
Into his bloody, or plaguy, or starved jaws;
Now he will seem to spare, and doth more waste,
Eating the best first, well preserved to last;
Now wantonly he spoils and eats us not,
But breaks off friends and lets us piecemeal rot.
Nor will this earth serve him; he sinks the deep,
Where harmless fish monastic silence keep,

1 women, 1609. 2 her virtue thinks, 1635, '39. 3 dished, 1635, '39.
II.— 9.

Who, were Death dead, by [1] rocs of living sand
Might sponge that element and make it land.
He rounds the air and breaks the hymnic notes
In birds', Heaven's choristers, organic throats,
Which (if they did not die) might seem to be
A tenth rank in the heavenly hierarchy.
O strong and long-lived Death, how cam'st thou in,
And how, without creation, didst begin?
Thou hast, and shalt see dead, before thou diest,
All the four monarchies and Antichrist.
How could I think thee nothing, that see now
In all this All, nothing else is but thou?
Our births and life, [2] vices and virtues, be
Wasteful consumptions, and degrees of thee.
For we, to live, our bellows wear and breath;
Nor are we mortal, dying, dead, but death.
And though thou beest (O mighty bird of prey)
So much reclaimed by God that thou must lay
All that thou kill'st at his feet, yet doth he
Reserve but few, and leaves the most to [3] thee;
And, of those few, now thou hast overthrown
One whom thy blow makes not ours, nor thine own;
She was more stories high; hopeless to come
To her soul, thou hast offered at her lower room.
Her soul and body was a king and court;
But thou hast both of captain missed and fort.
As houses fall not, though the king [4] remove,
Bodies of saints rest for their souls above.
Death gets 'twixt souls and bodies such a place
As sin insinuates 'twixt just men and grace;

1 the.   2 lives.   3 for.   4 kings.

Both work a separation, no divorce:
Her soul is gone to usher up her corse,
Which shall be almost another soul, for there
Bodies are purer than best souls are here.
Because in her her virtues did outgo
Her years, would'st thou, O emulous Death, do so,
And kill her young to thy loss? must the cost
Of beauty and wit, apt to do harm, be lost?
What though thou found'st her proof 'gainst sins of youth?
Oh, every age a diverse sin pursueth.
Thou should'st have stayed and taken better hold;
Shortly, ambitious; covetous, when old,
She might have proved; and such devotiön
Might once have strayed to superstitiön.
If all her virtues must have grown, yet might
Abundant virtue have bred a proud delight.
Had she persévered just, there would have bin
Some that would sin, misthinking she did sin;
Such as would call her friendship love, and feign
To sociäbleness a name profane,
Or sin by tempting, or, not daring that,
By wishing, though they never told her what.
Thus might'st thou have slain more souls, hadst thou not crost
Thyself, and, to triúmph, thine army lost.
Yet, though these ways be lost, thou hast left one,
Which is, immoderate grief that she is gone:
But we may scape that sin, yet weep as much;
Our tears are due because we are not such.
Some tears that knot of friends her death must cost,
Because the chain is broke, but [1] no link lost.

1 though.

ELEGY ON MISTRESS BOULSTRED.

1635.

DEATH, be not proud; thy hand gave not this blow,
Sin was her captive, whence thy power doth flow;
The executioner of wrath thou art,
But to destroy the just is not thy part.
Thy coming, terror, anguish, grief denounces;
Her happy state courage, ease, joy pronounces.
From out the crystal palace of her breast,
The clearer soul was called to endless rest,
(Not by the thundering voice wherewith God threats,
But as with crownèd saints in heaven he treats,)
And, waited on by angels, home was brought
To joy that it through many dangers sought;
The key of mercy gently did unlock
The doors 'twixt heaven and it, when life did knock.
    Nor boast the fairest frame was made thy prey,
Because to mortal eyes it did decay;
A better witness than thou art assures
That, though dissolved, it yet a space endures;
No dram thereof shall want or loss sustain,
When her best soul inhabits it again.
Go then to people cursed before they were,
Their souls in triumph to thy conquest bear.
Glory not thou thyself in these hot tears
Which our face, not for her, but our harm wears,

The mourning livery given by Grace, not thee,
Which wills our souls in these streams washed should be,
And on our hearts, her memory's best tomb,
In this her epitaph doth write thy doom.
Blind were those eyes saw not how bright did shine
Through flesh's misty veil those beams divine;
Deaf were the ears not charmed with that sweet sound
Which did i' the spirit's instructed voice abound;
Of flint the conscience did not yield and melt
At what in her last act it saw and felt.

Weep not nor grudge, then, to have lost her sight,
Taught thus,—our after-stay's but a short night;
But by all souls, not by corruption choked,
Let in high-raisèd notes that power be invoked;
Calm the rough seas by which she sails, to rest
From sorrows here, to a kingdom ever blest,
And teach this hymn of her with joy, and sing,
The grave no conquest gets, Death hath no sting.

ON HIMSELF.[1]

1635.

MADAM:

THAT I might make your cabinet my tomb,
   And for my fame, which I love next my soul,
Next to my soul provide the happiest room,
   Admit to that place this last funeral scroll.

1 This poem occurs twice in the edition of 1635, and subsequent editions. The
first time it appears it begins at "Madam," but ends at "carcases"; the second
time, it begins at "My fortune" and ends at "allow," as here. The two versions
differ slightly from each other.

II.—9*.

Others by wills give legacies, but I,
Dying, of you do beg a legacy.

My fortune and my choice [1] this custom break,
When we are speechless [2] grown, to make stones speak :
Though no stone tell thee what I was, yet thou
In my grave's inside seest [3] what thou art now:
Yet thou 'rt not yet so good; till death us [4] lay
To ripe and mellow here, [5] we are stubborn clay.
Parents make us earth, and souls dignify
Us to be glass; here to grow gold we lie.
Whilst in our souls sin bred and pampered is,
Our souls become worm-eaten carcases;
So we ourselves miraculously destroy;
Here bodies with less miracle enjoy
Such privileges, enabled here to scale
Heaven, when the trumpet's air shall them [6] exhale.
Hear this and mend thyself, and thou mend'st me,
By making me, being dead, do good for thee;
   And think me well composed, that I could now
   A last sick hour to syllables allow.

1 will.   2 senseless.   3 see.   4 us death.
5 thee, 1635, '39, '49, '54 ; there, 1669.   6 then, 1669.

ELEGY ON THE LORD C.[1]

1635.

SORROW, who[2] to this house scarce knew the way,
Is, oh! heir of it, our all is his prey.
This strange chance claims strange wonder, and to us
Nothing can be so strange as to weep thus.
'T is well, his life's loud-speaking works deserve,
And give praise too; our cold tongues could not serve:
'T is well he kept tears from our eyes before,
That to fit this deep ill we might have store.
Oh, if a sweet-brier climb up by a tree,
If to a paradise that transplanted be,
Or felled and burnt for holy sacrifice,
Yet that must wither which by it did rise,
As we for him dead.   Though no family
E'er rigged a soul for heaven's discovery,
With whom more venturers more boldly dare
Venture their states, with him in joy to share,
We lose, what all friends loved, him; he gains now
But life by death, which worst foes would allow,
If he could have foes, in whose practice grew
All virtues whose name subtle school-men knew.
What ease can hope that we shall see him beget,
When we must die first, and cannot die yet?

1 Lord Chancellor Ellesmere. He died 1617.
2 that, 1649, '54, '69.

His children are his pictures; Oh! they be
Pictures of him dead; senseless, cold as he.
Here needs no marble tomb; since he is gone,
He, and about him his, are turned to stone.

ELEGY.[1]

LANGUAGE, thou art too narrow and too weak
To ease us now; great sorrow[2] cannot speak;
If we could sigh out accents, and weep words!
Grief wears and lessens, that tears breath affords;
Sad hearts, the less they seem, the more they are,
(So guiltiest men stand mutest at the bar,)
Not that they know not, feel not their estate,
But extreme sense hath made them desperate;
Sorrow, to whom we owe all that we be,
Tyrant in the fifth and greatest monarchy,
Was 't that she did possess all hearts before,
Thou hast killed her, to make thy empire more?
Knew'st thou some would, that knew her not, lament,
As in a deluge perish th' innocent?
Was 't not enough to have that palace won,
But thou must raze it too, that was undone?
Hadst thou stayed there and looked out at her eyes,
All had adored thee that now from thee flies;

---

1 This poem has simply the title of *Elegie* in the edition of 1633.
In subsequent editions it was printed with the "Elegies" as
Elegy XI., and entitled *Death*. 2 sorrows.

For they let out more light than they took in,
They told not when, but did the day begin;
She was too sapphirine and clear for [1] thee;
Clay, flint, and jet now thy fit dwellings be:
Alas! she was too pure, but not too weak;
Whoe'er saw crystal ordnance but would break?
And if we be thy conquest, by her fall
Thou 'st lost thy end, for in her perish all,[2]
Or if we live, we live but to rebel,
They know her better now, that knew her well.[3]
If we should vapour out and pine and die,
Since she first went, that were not misery;
She changed our world with hers; now she is gone,
Mirth and prosperity is oppressiön,
For of all moral virtues she was all
That Ethics speak of virtues cardinal.
Her soul was Paradise; the Cherubin
Set to keep it was Grace; that kept out Sin;
She had no more than let in Death; for we
All reap consumption from one fruitful tree;
God took her hence lest some of us should love
Her, like that plant, him and his laws above;
And when we tears, he mercy shed in this,
To raise our minds to heaven where now she is,
Who, if her virtues would have let her stay,
We had had a saint, have now a holiday.
Her heart was that strange bush where sacred fire,
Religion, did not cónsume, but inspire

1 to, 1633.   2 in her we perish all.
3 That know her better now who knew her well.

Such piety, so chaste use of God's day,
That what we turn to feast, she turned to pray,
And did prefigure here in devout taste
The rest of her high saboath which shall last.
Angels did hand her up, who next God dwell,
For she was of that order whence most fell,
Her body ¹ left with us, lest some had said
She could not die, except they saw her dead ;
For from less virtue and less beauteousness
The gentiles framed them gods and goddesses ;
The ravenous earth, that now woos her to be
Earth too, will be a Lemnia, and the tree
That wraps that crystal in a wooden tomb,
Shall be took up spruce filled with diamond : ²
And we her sad glad friends all bear a part
Of grief, for all would waste ³ a stoic's heart.

AN HYMN TO THE SAINTS, AND TO MARQUESS HAMILTON.

To Sir Robert Carr.⁴

SIR,

   I PRESUME you rather try what you can do in me, than
what I can do in verse ; you know my uttermost when it
was best, and even then I did best, when I had least truth
for my subjects.   In this present case there is so much

---

¹ body 's.   ² filléd with amome (?—J. R. L.).   ³ break.
⁴ This name is not prefixed to the letter in the edition of 1633.

truth, as it defeats all poetry. Call therefore this paper by what name you will, and if it be not worthy of you nor of him, we will smother it, and be it your sacrifice.[1] If you had commanded me to have waited on his body to Scotland and preached there, I would have embraced your[2] obligation with much[3] alacrity. But I thank you that you would command me that which I was loather[4] to do, for even that hath given a tincture of merit to the obedience of

Your poor friend
and servant in Christ Jesus,
J. DONNE.

WHETHER that soul, which now comes up to you,
Fill any former rank or make a new,
Whether it take a name named there before
Or be a name itself and order more
Than was in heaven till now, (for may not he
Be so, if every several angel be
A kind alone?) whatever order grow
Greater by him in heaven, we do not so.
One of your orders grows by his access,
But by his loss grow all our orders less:
The name of father, master, friend, the name
Of subject and of prince, in one are[5] lame;
Fair mirth is damped, and conversation black,
The household widowed, and the Garter slack;
The chapel wants an ear, council a tongue,
Story a theme, and music lacks a song.

1 of him, nor of you, nor of me, smother it, and be that the
sacrifice. 2 the. 3 more. 4 loath. 5 is.

Blest order, that hath him! the loss of him
Gangrened all orders here; all lost a limb.
Never made body such haste to confess
What a soul was; all former comeliness
Fled in a minute, when the soul was gone,
And, having lost that beauty, would have none :
So fell our monasteries, in one [1] instant grown,
Not to less houses, but to heaps of stone;
So sent this [2] body that fair form it wore,
Unto the sphere of forms, and doth (before
His soul shall fill up his sepulchral stone)
Anticipate a resurrectiön;
For, as in his fame now his soul is here,
So in the form thereof his body 's there.

    And if, fair soul, not with first Innocents
Thy station be, but with the Penitents,
(And who shall dare to ask then, when I am
Dyed scarlet in the blood of that pure Lamb,
Whether that colour which is scarlet then,
Were black or white before in eyes of men ?)
When thou rememb'rest what sins thou didst find
Amongst those many friends now left behind,
And seest such sinners as they are with thee,
Got thither by repentance, let it be
Thy wish to wish all there, to wish them clean,
Wish him a David, her a Magdalen.

1 an.   2 his.

DIVINE POEMS.

DIVINE POEMS.

HOLY SONNETS.

LA CORONA.

1. Deign at my hands this crown of prayer and praise
Weaved in my low [1] devout meláncholy,
Thou, which of good hast, yea, art treasury,
All-changing unchanged Anciënt of days,
But do not with a vile crown of frail bays
Reward my Muse's white sincerity,
But what thy thorny crown gained, that give me,
A crown of glory which doth flower always.
The ends crown our works, but thou crown'st our ends,
For at our end [2] begins our endless rest;
The first last end, now zealously possest
With a strong sober thirst, my soul attends.
'T is time that heart and voice be lifted high,
Salvatiön to all that will is nigh.

ANNUNCIATION.

2. Salvatiön to all that will is nigh;
That All which always is all everywhere,

---

[1] lone. [2] ends.

Which cannot sin and yet all sins must bear,
Which cannot die, yet cannot choose but die,
Lo, faithful Virgin, yields himself to lie
In prison in thy womb; and though he there
Can take no sin, nor thou give, yet he 'll wear,
Taken from thence, flesh which death's force may try.
Ere by the spheres time was created, thou
Wast in his mind (who is thy son and brother),
Whom thou conceiv'dst conceived; yea, thou art now
Thy Maker's maker and thy Father's mother,
Thou hast light in dark, and shut'st in little room
Immensity cloistered in thy dear womb.

NATIVITY.

3. *Immensity, cloistered in thy dear womb,*
   Now leaves his well-beloved imprisonment;
   There he hath made himself to his intent
   Weak enough now into our world to come;
   But oh, for thee, for him, hath th' inn no room?
   Yet lay him in this[1] stall, and from the Orient
   Stars and wise men will travel to prevent
   Th' effects[2] of Herod's jealous general doom.
   Seest thou, my soul, with thy faith's eyes,[3] how he
   Which fills all place, yet none holds him, doth lie?
   Was not his pity towards thee wondrous high,
   That would have need to be pitíed by thee?
   Kiss him and with him into Egypt go
   With his kind mother who partakes thy woe.

1 his, 1669. 2 effect, *ibid.* 3 eye.

TEMPLE.

4. *With his kind mother who partakes thy woe,*
 Joseph, turn back ; see where your child doth sit
 Blowing, yea, blowing-out those sparks of wit,
 Which himself on the Doctors did bestow ;
 The Word but lately could not speak and, lo,
 It suddenly speaks wonders : whence comes it
 That all which was, and all which should be writ,
 A shallow-seeming child should deeply know ?
 His Godhead was not soul to his Manhood,
 Nor had time mellowed him to this ripeness ;
 But as, for one which hath a long task, 't is good
 With the sun to begin his business,
 He in his age's morning thus began
 By miracles exceeding power of man.

CRUCIFYING.

5. *By miracles exceeding power of man*
 He faith in some, envy in some begat,
 For, what weak spirits admire, ambitious hate ;
 In both affections many to him ran,
 But oh, the worst are most, they will and can,
 Alas ! and do, unto the immaculate,
 Whose creature Fate is, now prescribe a fate,
 Measuring self-life's infinity[1] to [a] span,
 Nay, to an inch. Lo, where condemnèd he
 Bears his own cross with pain, yet by and by,

1 infinite, 1669.

When it bears him, he must bear more and die.
Now thou art lifted up, draw me to thee,
And, at thy death giving such liberal dole,
Moist with one drop of thy blood my dry soul.

RESURRECTION.

6. *Moist with one drop of thy blood, my dry soul*
   Shall (though she now be in extreme degree
   Too stony-hard, and yet too fleshly) be
   Freed by that drop from being starved, hard, or foul,
   And life, by this death abled, shall control
   Death whom thy death slew ; nor shall to me
   Fear of first or last death bring misery,
   If in thy little [1] book my name thou enroll :
   Flesh in that long sleep is not putrefied,
   But made that there, of which, and for which, 't was,
   Nor can by other means be glorified.
   May then sin's sleep, and death soon from me pass,
   That, waked from both, I again-risen may
   Salute the last and everlasting day.

ASCENSION.

7. *Salute the last and everlasting day,*
   Joy at the uprising of this Sun and Son,
   Ye, whose just[2] tears or tribulatïon
   Have purely washed or burnt your drossy clay;
   Behold the Highest, parting hence away,

1 life book.   2 true.

Lightens the dark clouds which he treads upon;
Nor doth he by ascending show alone,
But first he, and he first, enters the way.
O strong Ram, which hast battered heaven for me,
Mild Lamb, which with thy blood hast marked the path,
Bright Torch, which shin'st that I the way may see,
Oh! with thy own blood quench thy own just wrath,
And, if thy holy Spirit my Muse did raise,
Deign at my hands this crown of prayer and praise.

HOLY SONNETS.

I.

1635.

THOU hast made me, and shall thy work decay?
Repair me now, for now mine end doth haste;
I run to Death, and Death meets me as fast,
And all my pleasures are like yesterday.
I dare not move my dim eyes any way,
Despair behind, and Death before doth cast
Such terror, and my feeble flesh doth waste
By sin in it which it towards hell doth weigh:
Only thou art above, and when towards thee
By thy leave I can look, I rise again;
But our old subtle foe so tempteth me
That not one hour myself I can sustain;
Thy grace may wing me to prevent his art,
And thou like adamant draw mine iron heart.

II.

As due by many titles, I resign
Myself to thee, O God.   First I was made
By thee and for thee, and, when I was decayed,
Thy blood bought that the which before was thine ;
I am thy son, made with thyself to shine,
Thy servant, whose pains thou hast still repaid,
Thy sheep, thine image, and, till I betrayed
Myself, a temple of thy Spirit divine.
Why doth the devil then usurp on me ?
Why doth he steal, nay, ravish that 's thy right ?
Except thou rise and for thine own work fight,
Oh! I shall soon despair, when I do [1] see
That thou lov'st mankind well, yet wilt not choose me,
And Satan hates me, yet is loth to lose me.

III.

1635.

Oh ! might those sighs and tears return again
Into my breast and eyes, which I have spent
That I might in this holy discontent
Mourn with some fruit as I have mourned in vain;
In mine idolatry what showers of rain
Mine eyes did waste ! what griefs my heart did rent !
That sufferance was my sin I now repent ;
'Cause I did suffer, I must suffer pain.

[1] shall.

The hydroptic drunkard and night-scouting thief,
The itchy lecher and self-tickling proud,
Have the remembrance of past joys for relief
Of coming ills.   To poor me is allowed
No ease; for long, yet vehement grief hath been
The effect and cause, the punishment and sin.

IV.

O MY black soul! now thou art summonëd
By sickness, Death's heráld and champion,
Thou art like a pilgrim which abroad hath done
Treason and durst not turn to whence he is fled,
Or like a thief which, till death's doom be read,
Wisheth himself delivered from prisón,
But, damned and haled to execution,
Wisheth that still he might be imprisonëd;
Yet grace, if thou repent, thou canst not lack;
But who shall give thee that grace to begin?
Oh, make thyself with holy mourning black,
And red with blushing as thou art with sin;
Or wash thee in Christ's blood which hath this might,
That, being red, it dies red souls to white.

V.

1635.

I AM a little world made cunningly
Of elements and an angelic spright,

II.— 10*.

But black sin hath betrayed to endless night
My world's both parts, and, oh! both parts must die.
You, which beyond that heaven which was most high,
Have found new spheres and of new land can write,
Pour new seas in mine eyes, that so I[1] might
Drown my world with my weeping earnestly,
Or wash it, if it must be drowned no more:
But, oh! it must be burnt; alas! the fire
Of lust and envy burnt it heretofore
And made it fouler: Let their flames retire,
And burn me, O Lord, with a fiery zeal
Of thee and thy house, which doth in eating heal.

VI.

THIS is my play's last scene; here heavens appoint
My pilgrimage's last mile, and my race,
Idly yet quickly run, hath this last pace,
My span's last inch, my minute's latest point,
And gluttonous death will instantly unjoint
My body and my[2] soul, and I shall sleep a space;
But my ever-waking part shall see that face,
Whose fear already shakes my every joint:
Then, as my soul to heaven, her first seat, takes flight,
And earth-born body in the earth shall dwell,
So fall my sins, that all may have their right,
To where they are bred and would press me, to hell.
Impute me righteöus, thus purged of evil,
For thus I leave the world, the flesh, the devil.

1 he, 1669.   2 body and soul.

VII.

At the round earth's imagined corners blow
Your trumpets, Angels, and arise, arise
From death, you numberless infinities
Of souls, and to your scattered bodies go
All whom the flood did, and fire shall, o'erthrow,[1]
All whom war, death, age, agues, tyrannies,
Despair, law, chance hath slain, and you whose eyes
Shall behold God and never taste death's woe ;
But let them sleep, Lord, and me mourn a space ;
For, if above all these my sins abound,
'T is late to ask abundance of thy grace,
When we are there.   Here on this lowly [2] ground
Teach me how to repent ; for that 's as good
As if thou had'st sealed my pardon with thy [3] blood.

VIII.

1635.

If faithful souls be alike glorified
As angels, then my father's soul doth see,
And adds this even to full felicity,
That valiantly I hell's wide mouth o'erstride :
But if our minds to these souls be descried
By circumstances and by signs that be
Apparent in us not immediately,
How shall my mind's white truth by them be tried ?

1 overthrow, 1669. 2 holy, *ibid.* 3 my, *ibid.*

They see idolatrous lovers weep and mourn,
And stile [1] blasphémous conjurers to call
On Jesus' name, and Pharisaical
Dissemblers feign devotiön.   Then turn,
O pensive soul, to God ; for he knows best
Thy grief, for he put it into my breast.

IX.

If poisonous minerals, and if that tree
Whose fruit threw death on else immortal us,
If lecherous goats, if serpents envious
Cannot be damned, alas ! why should I be ?
Why should intent or reason, born in me,
Make sins, else equal, in me more heinóus ?
And mercy being easy and glorious
To God, in his stern wrath why threatens he ?
But who am I that dare dispute with thee ?
O God, oh ! of thine only worthy blood
And my tears make a heavenly Lethean flood,
And drown in it my sins' black memory :
That thou remember them, some claim as debt ;
I think it mercy if thou wilt forget.

X.

Death, be not proud, though some have callëd thee
Mighty and dreadful, for thou art not so ;
For those whom thou think'st thou dost overthrow
Die not, poor Death, nor yet canst thou kill me.

[1] still (?).

From rest and sleep, which but thy pictures[1] be,
Much pleasure, then from thee much more must flow;
And soonest our best men with thee do go,
Rest of their bones, and soul's delivery.
Thou art slave to Fate, chance, kings, and desperate
      men,
And dost[2] with poison, war, and sickness dwell,
And poppy or charms can make us sleep as well
And better than thy stroke ; why swell'st thou then ?
One short sleep past, we wake eternally
And Death shall be no more; Death, thou shalt die.

XI.

Spit in my face, you Jews, and pierce my side,
Buffet and scoff, scourge and crucify me,
For I have sinned and sinned, and only he
Who could do no iniquity hath died:
But by my death cannot be satisfied
My sins which pass the Jews' impiety;
They killed once an inglorious man, but I
Crucify him daily, being now glorified.
Oh, let me then his strange love still admire:
Kings pardon, but he bore, our punishment;
And Jacob came, clothed in vile harsh attire,
But to supplant and with gainful intent;
God clothed himself in vile man's flesh, that so
He might be weak enough to suffer woe.

1 picture.   2 doth, 1633.

XII.

WHY are we by all creatures waited on ?
Why do the prodigal elements supply
Life and food to me, being more pure than I,
Simple,[1] and further from corruptiön ?
Why brook'st thou, ignorant horse, subjectiön ?
Why dost thou, bull and boar, so sillily
Dissemble weakness, and by one man's stroke die,
Whose whole kind you might swallow and feed upon ?
Weaker I am, woe is me ! and worse than you;
You have not sinned, nor need be timorous;
But wonder at a greater[2] wonder, for to us
Created nature doth these things subdue;
But their Creator, whom sin nor nature tied,
For us, his creatures and his foes, hath died.

XIII.

WHAT if this present were the world's last night ?
Mark in my heart, O Soul, where thou dost dwell,
The picture of Christ crucified, and tell
Whether his countenance can thee affright;
Tears in his eyes quench the amazing light,
Blood fills his frowns, which from his pierced head fell;
And can that tongue adjudge thee unto hell,
Which prayed forgiveness for his foes' fierce spite ?
No, no; but as in my idolatry
I said to all my profane mistresses,

1 simpler. 2 a greater, for to us.

Beauty, of pity, foulness only is
A sign of rigour, so I say to thee;
To wicked spirits are horrid shapes assigned,
This beauteous form assumes a piteous mind.

XIV.

BATTER my heart, three-personed God, for you
As yet but knock, breathe, shine, and seek to mend;
That I may rise and stand, o'erthrow me, and bend
Your force to break, blow, burn, and make me new.
I, like an usurped town to another due,
Labour to admit you, but oh, to no end;
Reason, your viceroy in me, me [1] should defend,
But is captíved, and proves weak or untrue;
Yet dearly I love you, and would be loved fain,
But am betrothed unto your enemy:
Divorce me, untie, or break that knot again,
Take me to you, imprison me, for I,
Except you enthral me, never shall be free,
Nor ever chaste, except you ravish me.

XV.

WILT thou love God, as he thee? then digest,
My Soul, this wholesome meditatiön,
How God the Spirit, by angels waited on
In heaven, doth make his temple in thy breast;

1 we, 1669.

The Father having begot a Son most blest,
And still begetting, (for he ne'er begun,)
Hath deigned to choose thee by adoptiön,
Coheir to his glory and Sabbath's endless rest.
And as a robbed man, which by search doth find
His stolen stuff sold, must lose or buy it again,
The Son[1] of glory came down and was slain,
Us, whom he had made and Satan stolen,[2] to unbind.
'T was much, that man was made like God before,
But, that God should be made like man, much more.

XVI.

FATHER, part of his double interest
Unto thy kingdom thy Son gives to me;
His jointure in the knotty Trinity
He keeps, and gives to me his death's conquést.
This Lamb, whose death with life the world hath blest,
Was from the world's beginning slain, and he
Hath made two wills which, with the legacy
Of his and thy kingdom,[3] do thy sons invest;
Yet such are these laws that men argue yet
Whether a man those statutes can fulfil;
None doth; but thy all-healing grace and Spirit
Revive again what law and letter kill:
Thy law's abridgment and thy last command
Is all, but love; Oh, let this last will stand!

1 sun. 2 stole. 3 thy kingdóm, thy sons.

ON THE BLESSED VIRGIN MARY.

1635.

In that, O Queen of queens, thy birth was free
From that which others doth of grace bereave,
When in their mother's womb they life receive,
God, as his sole-born daughter, lovèd thee.

To match thee like thy birth's nobility,
He thee his Spirit for his spouse did leave,
By whom thou didst his only Son conceive,
And so wast linked to all the Trinity.

Cease then, O queens that earthly crowns do wear,
To glory in the pomp of earthly things;
If men such high respects unto you bear,
Which daughters, wives, and mothers are of kings,
What honour can unto that Queen be done,
Who had your God for Father, Spouse, and Son?

THE CROSS.

Since Christ embraced the Cross itself, dare I,
His image, th' image of his Cross deny?
Would I have profit by the sacrifice,
And dare the chosen altar to despise?

It bore all other sins, but is it fit
That it should bear the sin of scorning it?
Who from the picture would avert his eye,
How would he fly his pains who there did die?
From me no pulpit, nor misgrounded law,
Nor scandal taken, shall this Cross withdraw;
It shall not, for it cannot; for the loss
Of this Cross were to me another cross;
Better were worse, for no afflictiön,
No cross is so extreme, as to have none.
Who can blot out the Cross, which th' instrument
Of God dewed on me in the Sacrament?
Who can deny me power and liberty
To stretch mine arms and mine own Cross to be?
Swim, and at every stroke thou art thy Cross;
The mast and yard make one, where seas do toss;
Look down, thou spiest out [1] crosses in small things;
Look up, thou seest birds raised on crossëd wings.
All the globe's frame and spheres is nothing else
But the meridian's crossing parallels.
Material crosses, then, good physic be,
But yet spiritual have chief dignity;
These for extracted chemic medicine serve,
And cure much better and as well preserve;
Then are you your own physic, or need none,
When stilled or purged by tribulatiön,
For, when that cross ungrudged unto you sticks,
Then are you to yourself a crucifix;

---

[1] our, 1669.

As perchance carvers do not faces make,
But that away, which hid them there, do take,
Let crosses so take what hid Christ in thee,
And be his image, or not his, but he.
But as oft alchemists do coiners prove,
So may a self-despising get self-love;
And then, as worst surfeits of best meats be,
So is pride issued from humility;
For 't is no child, but monster; therefore cross
Your joy in crosses, else 't is double loss.
And cross thy senses, else both they and thou
Must perish soon and to destruction bow;
For if the eye seek [1] good objects, and will take
No cross from bad, we cannot scape a snake.
So with harsh, hard, sour, stinking, cross the rest,
Make them indifferent; call nothing best. [2]
But most the eye needs crossing, that can roam
And move; to th' other th' objects [3] must come home.
And cross thy heart, for that in man alone
Pants downwards and hath palpitatiön;
Cross those dejections [4] when it downward tends,
And when it to forbidden heights pretends.
And as the brain through bony walls doth vent
By sutures, which a cross's form present,
So when thy brain works, ere thou utter it,
Cross and correct concúpiscence of wit.
Be covetous of crosses, let none fall;
Cross no man else, but cross thyself in all.

1 see, 1649, '54, '69. 2 Make them indifferent; all, nothing best.
3 To th' others objects must. 4 detorsions.

Then doth the Cross of Christ work faithfully
Within our hearts, when we love harmlessly
The Cross's pictures much, and with more care
That Cross's children, which our crosses are.

RESURRECTION.

Imperfect.

SLEEP, sleep, old sun, thou canst not have repast
As yet the wound thou took'st on Friday last;
Sleep then, and rest, the world may bear thy stay;
A better Sun rose before thee to-day,
Who, (not content to enlighten all that dwell
On the earth's face, as thou,) enlightened hell
And made the dark fires languish in that vale,
As at thy presence here our fires grow pale;
Whose body having walked on earth, and now
Hasting to Heaven, would, that he might allow
Himself unto all stations, and fill all,
For these three days become a mineral.
He was all gold when he lay down, but rose
All tincture, and doth not alone dispose
Leaden and iron wills to good, but is
Of power to make even sinful flesh like his.
Had one of those whose credulous piety
Thought that a soul one might discern and see

Go from a body, at this sepúlchre been,
And issuing from the sheet this body seen,
He would have justly thought this body a soul,
If not of any man, yet of the whole.

Desunt cetera.

THE ANNUNCIATION AND PASSION.

TAMELY, frail body,[1] abstain to-day; to-day
My soul eats twice, Christ hither and away;
She sees him man, so like God made in this,
That of them both a circle emblem is,
Whose first and last concur; this doubtful day
Of feast or fast Christ came and went away.
She sees him nothing twice at once, who is all;
She sees a cedar plant itself and fall;
Her Maker put to making, and the head
Of life at once not yet alive yet[2] dead;
She sees at once the Virgin-mother stay
Reclused at home, public at Golgotha;
Sad and rejoiced she 's seen at once, and seen
At almost fifty and at scarce fifteen;
At once a son is promised her and gone;
Gabriel gives Christ to her, he her to John;
Not fully a mother, she 's in orbity,
At once receiver and the legacy;

1 flesh.   2 and.

II.—11.

All this, and all between, this day hath shown,
Th' abridgment of Christ's story, which makes one
(As in plain maps the furthest West is East)
Of the angel's *Ave* and *Consummatum est.*
How well the Church, God's Court of Faculties,
Deals in sometimes and seldom joining these!
As by the self-fixed Pole we never do
Direct our course, but the next star thereto,
Which shows where the other is, and which we say
(Because it strays not far) doth never stray,
So God by his Church, nearest to him, we know,
And stand firm if we by her motion go;
His Spirit as[1] his fiery pillar doth
Lead, and his Church as cloud; to one end both.
This Church, by letting those days[2] join, hath shown
Death and conception in mankind is[3] one;
Or 't was in him the same humility,
That he would be a man and leave to be;
Or as creation he hath made, as God,
With the last judgment but one period,
His imitating spouse would join in one
Manhood's extremes: *He shall come, he is gone;*
Or as, though one blood-drop which thence did fall,
Accepted, would have served, he yet shed all,
So, though the least of his pains, deeds, or words,
Would busy a life, she all this day affords.
This treasure then in gross, my soul, up-lay,
And in my life retail it every day.

[1] and. [2] feasts. [3] are.

GOODFRIDAY, 1613, RIDING WESTWARD.

LET man's soul be a sphere, and then in this
The intelligence that moves, devotion is;
And as the other spheres, by being grown
Subject to foreign motion, lose their own,
And being by others hurried every day,
Scarce in a year their natural form obey,
Pleasure or business so our souls admit
For their first mover, and are whirled by it.
Hence is't that I am carried towards the West
This day, when my soul's form bends towards [1] the East,
There I should see a Sun by rising set,
And, by that setting, endless day beget;
But that Christ on this cross did rise and fall,
Sin had eternally benighted all.
Yet dare I almost be glad I do not see
That spectacle of too much weight for me.
Who sees God's face, that is self life, must die;
What a death were it then to see God die?
It made his own lieutenant, Nature, shrink,
It made his footstool crack, and the sun wink.
Could I behold those hands which span the poles
And tune all spheres at once, pierced with those holes?
Could I behold that endless height, which is
Zenith to us and our antipodes,
Humbled below us? or that blood, which is
The seat of all our souls, if not of his,

1 to.

Made dirt of dust? or that flesh, which was worn
By God for his apparel, ragg'd and torn?
If on these things I durst not look, durst I
Upon his miserable [1] mother cast mine eye,
Who was God's partner here, and furnished thus
Half of that sacrifice which ransomed us?
Though these things, as I ride, be from mine eye,
They are present yet unto my memory,
For that looks towards them; and thou look'st towards me,
O Saviour, as thou hang'st upon the tree;
I turn my back to thee, but to receive
Corrections, till thy mercies bid thee leave.
Oh, think me worth thine anger, punish me,
Burn off my rusts,[2] and my deformity;
Restore thine image so much by thy grace,
That thou may'st know me, and I 'll turn my face.

THE LITANY.

I. THE FATHER.

FATHER of Heaven and him by whom
  It, and us for it, and all else for us
  Thou mad'st and govern'st ever, come,
And re-create me, now grown ruinous:
    My heart is by dejection clay,
    And by self-murder red.
From this red earth, O Father, purge away

---

1 On his distressèd.   2 rust.

All vicious tinctures, that new fashionëd
I may rise up from death before I am dead.

II. THE SON.

O Son of God, who seeing two things,
Sin and Death, crept in, which were never made,
  By bearing one, triedst with what stings
The other could thine heritage invade;
    Oh, be thou nailed unto my heart,
    And crucified again;
Part not from it, though it from thee would part,
But let it be, by applying so thy pain,
Drowned in thy blood, and in thy passion slain.

III. THE HOLY GHOST.

O Holy Ghost, whose temple I
Am, but of mud walls and condensëd dust,
  And being sacrilegiously
Half-wasted with youth's fires of pride and lust,
    Must with new storms be weather-beat,
    Double in my heart thy flame,
Which let devout sad tears intend; and let
(Though this glass lantern, flesh, do suffer maim)
Fire, sacrifice, priest, altar be the same.

IV. THE TRINITY.

O blessed, glorious Trinity,
Bones to Philosophy, but milk to Faith,
II.—11*.

Which, as wise serpents, diversely
Most slipperiness, yet most entanglings, hath,
 As you distinguished, undistinct,
 By power, love, knowledge be,
Give me a[1] such self different instínct,
Of these let all me elemented be,
Of power to love, to know, you unnumbered Three.

V. THE VIRGIN MARY.

For that fair, blessed, Mother-maid
Whose flesh redeemed us, that she-cherubin
 Which unlocked paradise and made
One claim for innocence, and disseized sin,
 Whose womb was a strange heaven, for there
 God clothed himself and grew,
Our zealous thanks we pour. As her deeds were
Our helps, so are her prayers; nor can she sue
In vain, who hath such titles unto you.

VI. THE ANGELS.

And since this life our nonage is,
And we in wardship to thine angels be,
 Native in heaven's fair[2] palaces,
Where we shall be but denizened by thee;
 As th' earth, conceiving by the sun,
 Yields fair diversity,
Yet never knows which[3] course that light doth run,
So let me study that mine actions be
Worthy their sight, though blind in how they see.

1 Give me such. 2 heaven's palaces, 1649, '54, '69. 3 what.

VII.   THE PATRIARCHS.

AND let thy patriarchs' desire
(Those great-grandfathers of thy Church, which saw
    More in the cloud than we in fire,
Whom Nature cleared more, than us grace and law,
    And now in heaven still pray that we
    May use our new helps right)
Be sanctified,[1] and fructify in me;
Let not my mind be blinder by more light,
Nor Faith, by Reason added, lose her sight.

VIII.   THE PROPHETS.

THY eagle-sighted prophets, too,
(Which were thy Church's organs, and did sound
    That harmony which made of two
One law, and did unite, but not confound,—
    Those heavenly poets which did see
    Thy will, and it express
In rhythmic feet,) in common pray for me,
That I by them excuse not my excess
In seeking secrets or poeticness.

IX.   THE APOSTLES.

AND thy illustrious zodiac
Of twelve apostles which ingirt this All,
    (From whom whosoever do not take
Their light, to dark deep pits throw down and fall[2])

1 satisfied.   2 thrown down do fall.

As through their prayers thou hast let me know
That their books are divine,
May they pray still, and be heard, that I go
Th' old broad way in applying; oh, decline
Me, when my comment would make thy word mine.

X.   THE MARTYRS.

AND since thou so desirously
Didst long to die, that long before thou could'st,
   And long since thou no more could'st die,
Thou in thy scattered mystic body would'st
     In Abel die, and ever since
     In thine; let their blood come
To beg for us a discreet patiënce
Of death, or of worse life; for, oh! to some
Not to be martyrs is a martyrdom.

XI.   THE CONFESSORS.

THEREFORE with thee triúmpheth there
A virgin squadron of white cónfessors,
   Whose bloods betrothed, not married, were,
Tendered, not taken by those ravishers ;
     They know, and pray that we may know,
     In every Christiän
Hourly tempestuous persecutions grow ;
Tentations martyr us alive ; a man
Is to himself a Diocletiän.

XII. THE VIRGINS.

THE cold, white, snowy nunnery,
Which, as thy mother, their high abbess, sent
  Their bodies back again to thee,
As thou hadst lent them, clean and innocent,
  Though they have not obtained of thee,
  That or thy Church, or I,
Should keep, as they, our first integrity,
Divorce thou sin in us, or bid it die,
And call chaste widowhead virginity.

XIII. THE DOCTORS.

THY sacred ácademy[1] above
Of doctors, whose pains have unclasped and taught
  Both books of life to us, (for love
To know thy scriptures[2] tells us we are wrought[3]
  In thy other book,) pray for us there,
  That what they have misdone
Or missaid, we to that may not adhere ;
Their zeal may be our sin.   Lord, let us run
Mean ways, and call them stars, but not the sun.

XIV.

AND whilst this universal choir,
That church in triumph, this in warfare here,
  Warmed with one all-partaking fire
Of love that none be lost which cost thee dear,

1 The sacred academ.   2 the scriptures, 1649, '54; the scripture, 1669.   3 wrote.

Prays ceaselessly, and thou hearken too,
(Since to be graciöus
Our task is treble, to pray, bear, and do,)
Hear this prayer, Lord : O Lord, deliver us
From trusting in those prayers, though poured out thus.

XV.

FROM being anxious or secure,
Dead clods[1] of sadness or light squibs of mirth,
    From thinking that great courts immure
All or no happiness, or that this earth
      Is only for our prison framed,
      Or that thou art covetous
To them whom thou lovest, or that they are maimed
From reaching this world's sweet[2] who seek thee thus
With all their might, good Lord, deliver us.

XVI.

FROM needing danger, to be good,
From owing[3] thee yesterday's tears to-day,
    From trusting so much to thy blood,
That in that hope we wound our soul[4] away,
      From bribing thee with alms to excuse
      Some sin more burdenous,
From light affecting, in religion, news,
From thinking us all soul, neglecting thus
Our mutual duties, Lord, deliver us.

---

1 clouds.   2 sweets.   3 owning, 1669.   4 souls, *ibid.*

XVII.

FROM tempting Satan to tempt us
By our connivance or slack company,
  From measuring ill by viciöus
Neglecting to choke sin's spawn, vanity,
    From indiscreet humility,
    Which might be scandalous
And cast reproach on Christianity,
From being spies, or to spies pervious,
From thirst or scorn of flame,[1] deliver us.

XVIII.

DELIVER us for[2] thy descent
Into the Virgin, whose womb was a place
  Of middle kind, and thou being sent
To ungracious us, stayed'st at her full of grace,
    And through thy poor birth, where first thou
    Glorified'st poverty,
And yet soon after riches didst allow
By accepting kings' gifts in the Epiphany,
Deliver, and make us to both ways free.

XIX.

AND through[3] that bitter agony
Which is still[4] the agony of pious wits,
  Disputing what distorted thee
And interrupted evenness with fits,

1 fame. 2 through. 3 though, 1633. 4 still is.

And through thy free confessiön,
Though thereby they were then
Made blind so that thou might'st from them have gone,
Good Lord, deliver us, and teach us when
We may not, and we may, blind unjust men.

XX.

THROUGH thy submitting all to blows
Thy face, thy clothes[1] to spoil, thy fame to scorn,
   All ways which rage or justice knows,
And by which thou could'st show that thou wast born,
     And through thy gallant humbleness
     Which thou in death didst show,
Dying before thy soul they could express,
Deliver us from death, by dying so
To this world, ere this world do bid us go.

XXI.

WHEN senses, which thy soldiers are,
We arm against thee and they fight for sin,
   When want, sent but to tame, doth war,
And work despair a breach to enter in,
     When plenty, God's imáge and seal,
     Makes us idolatrous
And love it, not him whom it should reveal,
When we are moved to seem religiöus
Only to vent wit, Lord, deliver us.

[1] robes.

XXII.

In Churches, when the infirmity
Of him which speaks, diminishes the Word,
When magistrates do misapply
To us, as we judge, lay or ghostly sword,
    When plague, which is thine angel, reigns,
    Or wars, thy champions, sway,
When heresy, thy second deluge, gains,
In th' hour of death, the eve of last judgment day,
Deliver us from the sinister way.

XXIII.

Hear us, oh, hear us, Lord: to thee
A sinner is more music when he prays,
    Than spheres or angels' praises be
In panegyric Alleluïas,
    Hear us, for till thou hear us, Lord,
    We know not what to say;
Thine ear to our sighs, tears, thoughts, gives voice
        and word.
O thou, who Satan heard'st in Job's sick day,
Hear thyself now, for thou in us dost pray.

XXIV.

That we may change to evenness
This intermitting aguish piety,
    That snatching cramps of wickedness,
And apoplexies of fast sin may die,

That music of thy promises,
  Not threats in thunder, may
Awaken us to our just offices,
What in thy book thou dost, or creatures, say
That we may hear, Lord, hear us, when we pray.

XXV.

THAT our ears' sickness we may cure,
  And rectify those labyrinths aright,
    That we, by hearkening, not procure
Our praise, nor others' dispraise so invite,
    That we get not a slipperiness,
      And senselessly decline,
From hearing bold wits jest at kings' excess,
To admit the like of majesty divine,
That we may lock our ears, Lord, open thine.

XXVI.

THAT living law, the magistrate,
  Which, to give us and make us physic, doth
    Our vices often aggravate,   .
That preachers, taxing sin before her growth,
    That Satan, and invenomed men
      Which will,[1] if we starve, dine,
When they do most accuse us, may see then
Us to amendment hear them thee decline,
That we may open our ears, Lord, lock thine.

1 well, 1633.

XXVII.

That learning, thine ambassador,
From thine allegiänce we never tempt,
   That beauty, paradise's flower,
For physic made, from poison be exempt,
   That wit, born apt high good to do,
      By dwelling lazily
On Nature's nothing, be not nothing too,
That our affections kill us not, nor die,
Hear us weak echoes, O thou ear and cry.

XXVIII.

Son of God, hear us; and since thou,
By taking our blood, owest it us again,
   Gain to thyself or[1] us allow;
And let not both us and thyself be slain.
   O Lamb of God, which took'st our sin,
      Which could not stick to thee,
Oh, let it not return to us again,
But, patient and physician being free,
As sin is no thing, let it no where be.

[1] and.

UPON THE TRANSLATION OF THE PSALMS BY SIR PHILIP SYDNEY AND THE COUNTESS OF PEMBROKE HIS SISTER.

1635.

ETERNAL God, (for whom whoever dare
Seek new expressions, do the circle square
And thrust into strait corners of poor wit
Thee, who art cornerless and infinite,)
I would but bless thy name, not name thee now ;
And thy gifts are as infinite as thou ;
Fix we our praises therefore on this one,
That as thy blessed Spirit fell upon
These psalms' first author in a cloven tongue,
(For 't was a double power by which he sung
The highest matter in the noblest form),
So thou hast cleft that Spirit to perform
That work again, and shed it here upon
Two by their bloods, and by thy Spirit one,
A brother and a sister, made by thee
The organ, where thou art the harmony,
Two, that make one John Baptist's holy voice,
And who that psalm, *Now let the Isles rejoice*,
Have both translated and applied it too,
Both told us what, and taught us how to do.
They show us islanders our joy, our king,
They tell us why, and teach us how to sing,

Make all this All, three choirs, heaven, earth, and
    spheres;
The first, heaven, hath a song, but no man hears;
The spheres have music, but they have no tongue,
Their harmony is rather danced than sung;
But our third choir, to which the first gives ear,
(For angels learn by what the church does here,)
This choir hath all.   The organist is he
Who hath tuned God and Man, the organ we,
The songs are these which heaven's high holy Muse
Whispered to David, David to the Jews,
And David's súccessors in holy zeal,
In forms of joy and art, do re-reveal
To us so sweetly and sincerely, too,
That I must not rejoice as I would do,
When I behold that these psalms are become
So well attired abroad, so ill at home,
So well in chambers, in thy church so ill,
As I can scarce call that reformed until
This be reformed.   Would a whole state present
A lesser gift than some one man hath sent?
And shall our church unto our spouse and king
More hoarse, more harsh than any other, sing?
For *that* we pray, we praise thy name for *this*
Which by thy Moses and this Miriam is
Already done; and, as those psalms we call
(Though some have other authors) David's all,
So though some have, some may some psalms
    translate,
We thy Sydnean psalms shall celebrate,

II. —12.

And, till we come th' extemporal song to sing,
(Learned the first hour that we see the King
Who hath translated those translators,) may
These, their sweet learned labours, all the way
Be as our tuning, that, when hence we part,
We may fall in with them and sing our part.

ODE.

1635.

I.

VENGEANCE will sit above our faults; but till
        She there doth[1] sit,
We see her not, nor them.   Thus blind, yet still
We lead her way; and thus, whilst we do ill,
        We suffer it.

II.

Unhappy he whom youth makes not beware
        Of doing ill:
Enough we labour under age and care;
In number th' errors of the last place are
        The greatest still.

[1] do sit, 1649, '54, '69.

III.

Yet we, that should the ill we now begin,
     As soon repent,
(Strange thing!) perceive not; our faults are not seen
But past us; neither felt, but only in
     The punishment.

IV.

But we know ourselves least; mere outward shows
     Our minds so store,
That our souls, no more than our eyes, disclose
But form and colour. Only he who knows
     Himself, knows more.

TO MR. TILMAN, AFTER HE HAD TAKEN ORDERS.

1635.

THOU, whose diviner soul hath caused thee now
To put thy hand unto the holy plough,
Making lay scornings of the ministry
Not an impediment, but victory,
What bring'st thou home with thee? how is thy mind
Affected since the vintage? Dost thou find
New thoughts and stirrings in thee? and, as steel
Touched with a loadstone, dost new motions feel?

Or as a ship, after much pain and care,
For iron and cloth brings home rich Indian ware,
Hast thou thus trafficked, but with far more gain
Of noble goods, and with less time and pain?
Thou art the same materials as before,
Only the stamp is changëd, but no more;
And as new-crownëd kings alter the face,
But not the money's substance, so hath grace
Changed only God's old image by creation,
To Christ's new stamp, at this thy coronation;
Or as we paint angels with wings because
They bear God's message and proclaim his laws,
Since thou must do the like, and so must move,
Art thou new-feathered with celestial love?
Dear, tell me where thy purchase lies, and show
What thy advantage is above, below;
But if thy gainings do surmount expression,
Why doth the foolish world scorn that profession
Whose joys pass speech? Why do they think unfit
That gentry should join families with it,
As if their day were only to be spent
In dressing, mistressing, and compliment?
Alas, poor joys, but poorer men, whose trust
Seems richly placëd in sublimëd dust!
(For such are clothes and beauty, which, though gay,
Are, at the best, but of sublimëd clay.)
Let then the world thy calling disrespect,
But go thou on, and pity their neglect.
What function is so noble as to be
Ambassador to God and destiny?

To open life ? to give kingdóms to more
Than kings give dignities? to keep heaven's door?
Mary's prerogative was to bear Christ ; so
'T is preachers' to convey him ; for they do,
As angels out of clouds, from pulpits speak,
And bless the poor beneath, the lame, the weak.
If then th' astronomers, whereas they spy
A new-found star, their optics magnify,
How brave are those, who with their engine can
Bring man to heaven, and heaven again to man !
These are thy titles and preëminences,
In whom must meet God's graces, men's offences ;
And so the heavens, which beget all things here,
And the earth, our mother, which these things doth bear,
Both these in thee are in thy calling knit,
And make thee now a blest hermaphrodite.

A HYMN TO CHRIST,

AT THE AUTHOR'S LAST GOING INTO GERMANY.

In what torn ship soever I embark,
That ship shall be my emblem of thy Ark ;
What sea soever swallow me, that flood
Shall be to me an emblem of thy blood ;
Though thou with clouds of anger do disguise
Thy face, yet through that mask I know those eyes,
   Which, though they turn away sometimes,
     They never will despise.

II.—12*

I sacrifice this island unto thee,
And all whom I loved there [1] and who loved me;
When I have put our seas [2] 'twixt them and me,
Put thou thy seas [3] betwixt my sins and thee.
As the tree's sap doth seek the root below
In winter, in my winter now I go
   Where none but thee, th' eternal root
    Of true love I may know.

Nor thou, nor thy religion, dost control
The amorousness of an harmonious soul;
But thou would'st have that love thyself: as thou
Art jealous, Lord, so I am jealous now.
Thou lov'st not, till from loving more thou free
My soul: whoever gives, takes liberty:
   Oh, if thou car'st not whom I love,
    Alas, thou lov'st not me.

Seal then this bill of my divorce to all
On whom those fainter beams of love did fall;
Marry those loves, which in youth scattered be
On fame, [4] wit, hopes (false mistresses) to thee.
Churches are best for prayer that have least light;
To see God only, I go out of sight;
   And to scape stormy days, I choose
    An everlasting night.

---

[1] I love here and who love me. [2] this flood. [3] blood. [4] face.

THE LAMENTATIONS OF JEREMY.

FOR THE MOST PART ACCORDING TO TREMELIUS.[1]

CHAPTER I.

1. How sits this city, late most populous,
   Thus solitary, and like a widow thus?
   Amplest of nations, queen of provinces,
   She was, who now thus tributary is.

2. Still in the night she weeps, and her tears fall
   Down by her cheeks along, and none of all
   Her lovers comfort her; perfidiously
   Her friends have dealt, and now are enemy.

3. Unto great bondage and afflictiöns
   Judah is captive led; those natiöns
   With whom she dwells, no place of rest afford;
   In straits she meets her persecutor's sword.

4. Empty are the gates of Sion, and her ways
   Mourn because none come to her solemn days;
   Her priests do groan, her maids are comfortless;
   And she 's unto herself a bitterness.

5. Her foes are grown her head and live at peace,
   Because, when her transgressions did increase,
   The Lord strook her with sadness: th' enemy
   Doth drive her children to captivity.

---

1 Tremellius, 1639, '49, '54, '69.

⁶· From Sion's daughter is all beauty gone ;
Like harts, which seek for pasture and find none,
Her princes are : and now before the foe,
Which still pursues them, without strength they go.

⁷· Now in their days of tears, Jerusalem
(Her men slain by the foe, none succouring them)
Remembers what of old she esteemëd most,
Whiles her foes laugh at her for what she hath lost.

⁸· Jerusalem hath sinned, therefóre is she
Removed, as women in uncleanness be :
Who honoured, scorn her, for her foulness they
Have seen ; herself doth groan, and turn away.

⁹· Her foulness in her skirts was seen, yet she
Remembered not her end ; miraculously
Therefóre she fell, none comforting : behold,
O Lord, my affliction, for the foe grows bold.

¹⁰· Upon all things where her delight hath been,
The foe hath stretched his hand ; for she hath seen
Heathen, whom thou command'st should not do so,
Into her holy sanctuary go.

¹¹· And all her people groan and seek for bread ;
And they have given, only to be fed,
All precious things wherein their pleasure lay :
How cheap I am grown, O Lord, behold, and weigh.

12. All this concerns not you who pass by me ;
Oh see, and mark if any sorrow be
Like to my sorrow which Jehovah hath
Done to me in the day of his fierce wrath ?

13. That fire which by himself is governëd,
He hath cast from heaven on my bones, and spread
A net before my feet, and me o'erthrown,
And made me languish all the day alone.

14. His hand [1] hath of my sins framëd a yoke
Which, wreathed and cast upon my neck, hath broke
My strength : the Lord unto those enemies
Hath given me, from whence [2] I cannot rise.

15. He under foot hath trodden in my sight
My strong men ; he did company invite [3]
To break my young men ; he the wine-press hath
Trod upon Judah's daughter in his wrath.

16. For these things do I weep ; mine eye, mine eye
Casts water out ; for he which should be nigh
To comfort me, is now departed far ;
The foe prevails, forlorn my children are.

17. There 's none, though Sion do stretch out her hand,
To comfort her ; it is the Lord's command,
That Jacob's foes girt him : Jerusalem
Is as an unclean woman amongst them.

1 His hands, 1649, '54, '69.　2 whom.　3 accite.

[18.] But yet the Lord is just and righteous still;
I have rebelled against his holy will:
O hear, all people, and my sorrow see,
My maids, my young men in captivity.

[19.] I callèd for my lovers then, but they
Deceived me, and my priests and elders lay
Dead in the city; for they sought for meat [1]
Which should refresh their souls, they could not get.[2]

[20.] Because I am in straits, Jehovah, see
My heart o'erturned,[3] my bowels muddy be;
Because I have rebelled so much, as fast
The sword without, as death within doth waste.

[21.] Of all which here I mourn, none comforts me;
My foes have heard my grief, and glad they be,
That thou hast done it; but thy promised day
Will come, when, as I suffer, so shall they.

[22.] Let all their wickedness appear to thee;
Do unto them, as thou hast done to me
For all my sins: the sighs [4] which I have had
Are very many, and my heart is sad.

CHAPTER II.

[1.] How over Sion's daughter hath God hung
His wrath's thick cloud! and from heaven hath flung

---

1 the sought-for meat (?).   2 and none could get.
3 returned, 1633.   4 sights, 1669.

To earth the beauty of Israel, and hath
Forgot his footstool in the day of wrath !

2. The Lord unsparingly hath swallowëd
All Jacob's dwellings, and demolishëd
To ground the strengths[1] of Judah, and profaned
The princes of the kingdom and the land.

3. In heat of wrath the horn of Israel he
Hath clean cut off and, lest the enemy
Be hindered, his right hand he doth retire,
But is towards Jacob all-devouring fire.

4. Like to an enemy he bent his bow,
His right hand was in posture of a foe,
To kill what Sion's daughter did desire,
'Gainst whom his wrath he pourëd forth like fire.

5. For like an enemy Jehovah is,
Devouring Israel and his palaces ;
Destroying holds, giving additiöns
To Judah's daughters' lamentatiöns.

6. Like to a garden-hedge he hath cast down
The place where was his congregatiön,
And Sion's feasts and Sabbaths are forgot ;
Her king, her priest, his wrath regardeth[2] not.

7. The Lord forsakes his altar and detests
His sanctuary ; and in the foes' hands rests

1 strength. 2 regarded not, 1669.

His palace and the walls in which their cries
Are heard as in the true solemnities.

8. The Lord hath cast a line, so to confound
And level Sion's walls unto the ground ;
He draws not back his hand which doth o'erturn
The wall and rampart which together mourn.

9. Their [1] gates are sunk into the ground, and he
Hath broke the bar ; their king and princes be
Amongst the heathen, without law ; nor there
Unto their [2] prophets doth the Lord appear.

10. There Sion's elders on the ground are placed,
And silence keep ; dust on their heads they cast ;
In sackcloth have they girt themselves, and low
The virgins towards ground their heads do throw.

11. My bowels are grown muddy, and mine eyes
Are faint with weeping, and my liver lies
Poured out upon the ground for misery
That sucking children in the streets do die.

12. When they had cried unto their mothers, Where
Shall we have bread and drink ? they fainted there,
And in the street like wounded persons lay
Till 'twixt their mother's breasts they went away.

13. Daughter Jerusalem, oh ! what may be
A witness or comparison for thee ?

[1] The. [2] the, 1669.

Sion, to ease thee, what shall I name like thee?
Thy breach is like the sea; what help can be?

14. For thee[1] vain foolish things thy prophets sought;
Thee thine iniquities they have not taught,
Which might disturn[2] thy bondage, but for thee
False burthens and false causes they would see.

15. The passengers do clap their hands and hiss
And wag their head at thee and say, Is this
That city which so many men did call
Joy of the earth and perfectest of all?

16. Thy foes do gape upon thee, and they hiss
And gnash their teeth and say, Devour we this,
For this is certainly the day which we
Expected and which now we find and see.

17. The Lord hath done that which he purposèd;
Fulfilled his word, of old determinèd;
He hath thrown down and not spared, and thy foe
Made glad above thee, and advanced him so.

18. But now their hearts against[3] the Lord do call,
Therefore, O walls of Sion, let tears fall
Down like a river, day and night; take thee
No rest, but let thine eye incessant be.

19. Arise, cry in the night, pour, for[4] thy sins,
Thy heart, like water, when the watch begins;

1 For the, 1633, '09. 2 dis-urn, 1069. 3 unto. 4 pour out.

Lift up thy hands to God lest children die
Which, faint for hunger, in the streets do lie.

20. Behold, O Lord, consider unto whom
Thou hast done this; what, shall the women come
To eat their children of a span? shall thy
Prophet and priest be slain in sanctuary?

21. On ground in streets the young and old do lie,
My virgins and young men by sword do die;
Them in the day of thy wrath thou hast slain,
Nothing did thee from killing them contain.

22. As to a solemn feast, all whom I feared
Thou call'st about me: when his [1] wrath appeared,
None did remain or scape; for those which I
Brought up did perish by mine enemy.

CHAPTER III.

1. I AM the man which have affliction seen,
Under the rod of God's wrath having been,
2. He hath led me to darkness, not to light,
3. And against me all day his hand doth fight.

4. He hath broke my bones, worn out my flesh and skin,
5. Built up against me, and hath girt me in
With hemlock and with labour, 6. and set me
In dark as they who dead forever be.

---

1 thy.

7. He hath hedged me lest I scape, and added more
To my steel fetters, heavier than before.
8. When I cry out he outshuts my prayer, 9. and hath
Stopped with hewn stone my way, and turned my path.

10. And like a lion hid in secrecy,
Or bear which lies in wait, he was to me ;
11. He stops my way, tears me made desolate,
12. And he makes me the mark he shooteth at.

13. He made the children of his quiver pass
Into my reins. 14. I with my people was
All the day long a song and mockery.
15. He hath filled me with bitterness, and he

Hath made me drunk with wormwood. 16. He
hath burst
My teeth with stones, and covered me with dust,
17. And thus my soul far off from peace was set,
And my prosperity I did forget.

18. My strength, my hope (unto myself I said)
Which from the Lord should come, is perishëd.
19. But when my mournings I do think upon,
My wormwood, hemlock, and afflictiön,

20. My soul is humbled in remembering this,
21. My heart considers, therefore hope there is.
22. 'T is God's great mercy we are not utterly
Consumed, for his compassions do not die ;

23. For every morning they renewèd be,
For great, O Lord, is thy fidelity.
24. The Lord is, saith my soul, my portiön,
And therefore in him will I hope alone.

25. The Lord is good to them who on him rely,
And to the soul that seeks him earnestly.
26. It is both good to trust, and to attend
The Lord's salvatiön unto the end.

27. 'T is good for one his yoke in youth to bear ;
28. He sits alone, and doth all speech forbear,
Because he hath borne it ; 29. and his mouth he lays
Deep in the dust, yet then in hope he stays.

30. He gives his cheeks to whosoever will
Strike him, and so he is reproachèd still.
31. For not forever doth the Lord forsake,
32. But when he hath struck with sadness, he doth take

Compassion, as his mercy is infinite,
33. Nor is it with his heart, that he doth smite ;
34. That under foot the prisoners stampèd be,
35. That a man's right the judge himself doth see

To be wrong [1] from him, 36. that he subverted is
In his just cause, the Lord allows not this :
37. Who then will say, that aught doth come to pass,
But that which by the Lord commanded was ?

38. Both good and evil from his mouth proceeds ;
39. Why then grieves any man for his misdeeds ?

1 wrung.

⁴⁰· Turn we to God, by trying out our ways;
⁴¹· To him in heaven our hands with hearts upraise.

⁴²· We have rebelled, and fallen away from thee;
Thou pardon'st not, ⁴³· usest no clemency,
Pursuest us, kill'st us, coverest us with wrath,
⁴⁴· Cover'st thyself with clouds, that our prayer hath

No power to pass; ⁴⁵· and thou hast made us fall
As refuse and off-scouring to them all.
⁴⁶· All our foes gape at us. ⁴⁷· Fear and a snare,
With ruin and with waste, upon us are.

⁴⁸· With water¹ rivers doth mine eye o'erflow
For ruin of my people's daughters so;
⁴⁹· Mine eye doth drop down tears incessantly,
⁵⁰· Until the Lord look down from heaven to see.

⁵¹· And for my city-daughters' sake, mine eye
Doth break mine heart. ⁵²· Causeless mine enemy
Like a bird chased me. ⁵³· In a dungeon
They have shut my life, and cast me on a stone.

⁵⁴· Waters flowed o'er my head; then thought I, I am
Destroyed; ⁵⁵· I callèd, Lord, upon thy name,
Out of the pit, ⁵⁶· and thou my voice didst hear;
Oh! from my sigh² and cry stop not thine ear.

⁵⁷· Then when I called upon thee, thou drew'st near
Unto me, and saidst unto me, "Do not fear."

¹ watry. ² sight, 1669.

^{58.} Thou, Lord, my soul's cause handled hast, and thou
Rescuest my life. ^{59.} O Lord, do thou judge now,

Thou heard'st my wrong, ^{60.} their vengeance all they
 have wrought,
^{61.} How they reproached, thou hast heard, and what they
 thought,
^{62.} What their lips uttered which against me rose,
And what was ever whispered by my foes.

^{63.} I am their song, whether they rise or sit ;
^{64.} Give them rewards, Lord, for their working fit,
^{65.} Sorrow of heart, thy curse, ^{66.} and with thy might
Follow, and from under heaven destroy them quite.

CHAPTER IV.

^{1.} How is the gold become so dim ! How is
Purest and finest gold thus changed to this!
The stones, which were stones of the sanctuary,
Scattered in corners of each street do lie.

^{2.} The precious sons of Sion, which should be
Valued at ¹ purest gold, how do we see
Low-rated now, as earthen pitchers, stand,
Which are the work of a poor potter's hand !

^{3.} Even the sea-calfs draw their breasts and give
Suck to their young ; my people's daughters live,
By reason of the foe's great cruelness,
As do the owls in the vast wilderness.

1 as, 1649, '54, '69.

4. And when the sucking child doth strive to draw
His tongue for thirst cleaves to his upper jaw ;
And when for bread the little children cry
There is no man that doth them satisfy.

5. They which before were delicately fed
Now in the streets forlorn have perishèd,
And they which ever were in scarlet clothed
Sit and embrace the dunghills which they loathed.

6. The daughters of my people have sinned more
Than did the town of Sodom sin before ;
Which being at once destroyed, there did remain
No hands amongst them to vex them again.

7. But heretofore purer her Nazarite
Was than the snow, and milk was not so white ;
As carbuncles did their pure bodies shine,
And all their polishedness was Seraphine.[1]

8. They are darker now than blackness, none can know
Them by the face as through the street they go,
For now their skin doth cleave unto their bone,
And witherèd is like to dry wood grown.

9. Better by sword than famine 't is to die,
And better through-pierced than by[2] penury ;
10. Women, by nature pitiful, have eat
Their children (dressed with their own hand) for meat.

1 saphirine.　2 through.

^{11.} Jehovah here fully accomplished hath
His indignation, and poured forth his wrath ;
Kindled a fire in Sion which hath power
To eat, and her foundations to devour.

^{12.} Nor would the kings of the earth, nor all which live
In the inhabitable world believe,
That any adversary, any foe
Into Jerusalem should enter so.

^{13.} For the priests' sins, and prophets' which have shed
Blood in the streets, and the just murther̈ed ;
^{14.} Which, when those men whom they made blind did
        stray
Thorough[1] the streets defil̈ed by the way

With blood, the which impossible it was
Their garments[2] should scape touching as they pass,
^{15.} Would cry aloud, "Depart, defil̈ed men !
Depart, depart, and touch us not," and then

They fled and strayed and with the Gentiles were,
Yet told their friends they should not long dwell there ;
^{16.} For this they are scattered by Jehovah's face,
Who never will regard them more ; no grace

Unto their[3] old men shall the[4] foe afford,
Nor, that they are priests, redeem them from the sword.
^{17.} And we as yet, for all these miseries
Desiring our vain help, consume our eyes ;

1 through, 1669. 2 garment. 3 the, 1649, '54, '69. 4 their, *ibid.*

And such a natiön as cannot save,
We in desire and speculation have.

18. They hunt our steps, that in the streets we fear
To go; our end is now approachëd near,

Our days accomplished are, this the last day;
Eagles of heaven are not so swift as they
19. Which follow us; o'er mountain 1-tops they fly
At us, and for us in the desert lie.

20. The anointed Lord, breath of our nostrils, he
Of whom we said, under his shadow we
Shall with more ease under the heathen dwell,
Into the pit which these men diggëd fell.

21. Rejoice, O Edom's daughter; joyful be
Thou which 2 inhabit'st her; 3 for unto thee
This cup shall pass, and thou with drunkenness
Shalt fill thyself and show thy nakedness.

22. And then thy sins, O Sion, shall be spent;
The Lord will not leave thee in banishment:
Thy sins, O Edom's daughter, he will see,
And for them pay thee with captivity.

CHAPTER V.

1. REMEMBER, O Lord, what is fallen on us;
See and mark how we are reproachëd thus.
2. For unto strangers our possessiön
Is turned, our houses unto aliens gone,

---

1 mountains, *ibid.* 2 that. 3 Uz.

II.—13*

3. Our mothers are become as widows, we
As orphans all, and without fathers be ;
4. Waters which are our own we drunk,[1] and pay ;
And upon our own wood a price they lay ;

5. Our persecutors on our necks do sit,
They make us travail, and not intermit ;
6. We stretch our hands unto th' Egyptiäns
To get us bread ; and to the Assyrians.

7. Our fathers did these sins and are no more,
But we do bear the sins they did before.
8. They are but servants which do rule us thus,
Yet from their hands none would deliver us.

9. With danger of our life our bread we gat,
For in the wilderness the sword did wait ;
10. The tempests of this famine we lived in
Black as an oven[2] coloured had our skin.

11. In Judah's cities they the maids abused
By force, and so women in Sion used ;
12. The princes with their hands they hung ; no grace
Nor honour gave they to the elder's face.

13. Unto the mill our young men carried are,
And children fell under the wood they bare,
14. Elders the gates, youth did their songs forbear,
Gone was our joy, our dancings mournings were.

1 drink. 2 ocean, 1633.

^{15.} Now is the crown fallen from our head ; and woe
Be unto us, because we have sinnëd so.
^{16.} For this our hearts do languish, and for this
Over our eyes a cloudy dimness is,

^{17.} Because Mount Sion desolate doth lie,
And foxes there do go at liberty.
^{18.} But thou, O Lord, art ever, and thy throne
From generation to generatiön.

^{19.} Why should'st thou forget us eternally ?
Or leave us thus long in this misery ?
^{20.} Restore us, Lord, to thee, that so we may
Return, and, as of old, renew our day.

^{21.} For oughtest thou, O Lord, despise us thus,
^{22.} And to be utterly enraged at us?

HYMN TO GOD, MY GOD, IN MY SICKNESS.

1635.

Since I am coming to that holy room,
    Where with thy[1] choir of saints for evermore
I shall be made thy music, as I come,
    I tune the instrument here at the door,
    And, what I must do then, think here before.

1 the, 1639, '49, '54, '69.

Whilst my physicians by their love are grown
Cosmographers, and I, their map, who lie
Flat on this bed, that by them may be shown
That this is my South West discovery
Per fretum febris, by these straits to die,

I joy that in these straits I see my West;
For, though those currents yield return to none,
What shall my West hurt me? As West and East
In all flat maps (and I am one) are one,
So death doth touch the resurrectiön.

Is the Pacific Sea my home? Or are
The eastern riches? Is Jerusalem,
Anyan, and Magellan, and Gibraltár
(All straits, and none but straits are ways to them)
Whether where Japhet dwelt, or Cham, or Shem?

We think that Paradise and Calvary,
Christ's cross and Adam's tree, stood in one place;
Look, Lord, and find both Adams met in me;
As the first Adam's sweat surrounds my face,
May the last Adam's blood my soul embrace.

So in his purple wrapped receive me, Lord,
By these his thorns give me his other crown;
And as to others' souls I preached thy word,
Be this my text, my sermon to mine own,
Therefore, that he may raise, the Lord throws down.

A HYMN TO GOD THE FATHER.

I.

WILT thou forgive that sin where I begun,
  Which was my sin though it were done before?
Wilt thou forgive that sin through which I run
  And do run still, though still I do deplore?
When thou hast done, thou hast not done,
    For I have more.

II.

Wilt thou forgive that sin which I have won
  Others to sin, and made my sin [1] their door?
Wilt thou forgive that sin which I did shun
  A year or two, but wallowed in a score?
When thou hast done, thou hast not done,
    For I have more.

III.

I have a sin of fear, that when I have spun
  My last thread I shall perish on the shore;
But swear by thyself, that at my death thy Son
  Shall shine as he shines now and heretofore;
And having done that, thou hast done,
    I fear no more.

[1] sins, 1639, '49, '54, '69.

TO MR. GEORGE HERBERT, WITH ONE OF MY
SEALS[1] OF THE ANCHOR AND CHRIST.

1650.

Qui prius assuetus serpentum fasce tabellas·
   Signare (hæc nostræ symbola parva domus),
Adscitus domui Domini, patrioque relicto
   Stemmate, nanciscor stemmata jure nova.
Hinc mihi Crux, primo quæ fronti impressa lavacro,
   Finibus extensis Anchora facta patet.
Anchoræ in effigiem Crux tandem desinit ipsam,
   Anchora fit tandem Crux tolerata diu.
Hoc tamen ut fiat, Christo vegetatur ab ipso
   Crux, et ab affixo est Anchora facta Iesu.
Nec natalitiis penitus serpentibus orbor;
   Non ita dat Deus ut auferat ante data.
Qua sapiens, dos est; qua terram lambit et ambit,
   Pestis; at in nostra fit medicina Cruce
Serpens, fixa Cruci si sit natura, Crucique
   A fixo nobis Gratia tota fluat.
Omnia cum Crux sint, Crux Anchora fixa, sigillum
   Non tam dicendum hoc quam catechismus erit.
Mitto nec exigua exigua sub imagine dona,
   Pignora amicitiæ et munera, vota, preces.
Plura tibi accumulet sanctus cognominis Ille,
   Regia qui flavo dona sigillat equo.

                                       I. D.

1 seal, 1650, '54, '69.

TRANSLATION OF THE PRECEDING.

A SHEAF of snakes used heretofore to be
My seal, the crest of our poor family ;
Adopted in God's family, and so
Our old coat lost, unto new arms I go.
The cross (my seal at baptism) spread below,
Does by that form into an anchor grow.
Crosses grow anchors ; bear, as thou should'st do,
Thy cross, and that cross grows an anchor too.
But he that makes our crosses anchors thus,
Is Christ, who there is crucified for us.
Yet may I, with this, my first serpents hold ;
God gives new blessings, and yet leaves the old ;
The serpent may, as wise, my pattern be ;
My poison, as he feeds on dust that 's me ;
And as he rounds the earth to murder sure,
My death he is ; but on the cross, my cure.
Crucify nature then, and then implore
All grace from him crucified there before.
When all is cross, and that cross anchor grown,
This seal 's a catechism, not a seal alone.
Under that little seal great gifts I send,
Works and prayers, pawns, and fruits of a friend.
And may that saint, which rides in our Great Seal,
To you, who bear his name, great bounties deal.

AMICISSIMO ET MERITISSIMO BEN. JONSON.

IN VULPONEM.

1650.

Quod arte ausus es hic tua, Poeta,
Si auderent hominum Deique juris
Consulti, veteres sequi æmularierque,
O omnes saperemus ad salutem.
His sed sunt veteres araneosi ;
Tam nemo veterum est sequutor, ut tu,
Illos quod sequeris, novator audis.
Fac tamen quod agis, tuique prima
Libri canitie induantur hora ;
Nam chartis pueritia est neganda,
Nascanturque[1] senes oportet illi
Libri, queis dare vis perennitatem.
Priscis ingenium facit laborque
Te parem ; hos superes, ut et futuros
Ex nostra vitiositate sumas,[2]
Qua priscos superamus et futuros.

I. D.

1 nascunturque, 1650, '54.   2 sumes, 1654.

DE LIBRO, CUM MUTUARETUR, IMPRESSO, DOMI A PUERIS FRUSTRATIM LACERATO, ET POST REDDITO MANUSCRIPTO.

DOCTISSIMO AMICISSIMOQUE V. D. D. ANDREWS.

1635.

Parturiunt madido quæ nixu præla, recepta,
Sed quæ scripta manu sunt, veneranda magis.
Transiit in Sequanam Mœnus, victoris in ædes,
Et Francofurtum, te revehente, meat.
Qui liber in pluteos blattis cinerique relictos,
Si modo sit præli sanguine tinctus, abit,
Accedat calamo scriptus, reverenter habetur,
Involat et veterum scrinia summa Patrum.
Dicat Apollo modum, pueros infundere libro
Nempe vetustatem canitiemque novo.
Nil mirum, medico pueros de semine natos
Hæc nova fata libro posse dedisse novo.
Si veterem faciunt pueri, qui nuperos, annon
Ipse pater juvenem me dabit arte senem?
Hei miseris senibus! nos vertit dura senectus
Omnes in pueros, neminem at in juvenem.
Hoc tibi servasti præstandum, Antique Dierum,
Quo viso et vivit et juvenescit Adam.
Interea infirmæ fallamus tædia vitæ
Libris et cœlorum æmula amicitia.
Hos inter, qui a te mihi redditus, iste libellus
Non mihi tam charus, tam meus, ante fuit.

I. D.

ELEGIES UPON THE AUTHOR.

ELEGIES UPON THE AUTHOR.

TO THE MEMORY OF MY EVER DESIRED FRIEND DOCTOR DONNE.

To have lived eminent in a degree
Beyond our loftiest flights, that is, like thee,
Or t' have had too much merit, is not safe,
For such excesses find no epitaph.
At common graves we have poetic eyes
Can melt themselves in easy elegies,
Each quill can drop his tributary verse,
And pin it, like the hatchments, to the hearse ;
But at thine, poem or inscriptiön
(Rich soul of wit and language !) we have none.
Indeed a silence does that tomb befit
Where is no herald left to blazon it.
Widowed invention justly doth forbear
To come abroad, knowing thou art not here,
Late her great patron, whose prerogative
Maintained and clothed her so, as none alive
Must now presume to keep her at thy rate,
Though he the Indies for her dower estate.

Or else that awful fire which once did burn
In thy clear brain, now fall'n into thy urn
Lives there to fright rude empirics from thence,
Which might profane thee by their ignorance.
Whoever writes of thee and in a style
Unworthy such a theme, does but revile
Thy precious dust, and wake a learnèd spirit
Which may revenge his rapes upon thy merit ;
For all a low-pitched fancy can devise
Will prove, at best, but hallowed injuries.

    Thou, like the dying swan, didst lately sing
Thy mournful dirge in audience of the King ;
When pale looks and faint accents of thy breath
Presented so to life that piece of death,
That it was feared and prophesied by all,
Thou thither cam'st to preach thy funeral.
Oh! hadst thou in an elegiac knell
Rung out unto the world thine own farewell,
And in thy high victorious numbers beat
The solemn measure of thy grieved retreat,
Thou mightst the poets' service now have missed
As well as then thou didst prevent the priest,
And never to the world beholding be
So much as for an epitaph for thee.

    I do not like the office.   Nor is it fit
Thou, who didst lend our age such sums of wit,
Shouldst now re-borrow from her bankrupt mine
That ore to bury thee which once was thine.
Rather still leave us in thy debt ; and know
(Exalted soul !) more glory 't is to owe

Unto thy hearse what we can never pay,
Than with embaséd coin those rites defray.
Commit we then thee to thyself : nor blame
Our drooping loves, which thus to thy own fame
Leave thee executor ; since, but thine own,
No pen could do thee justice, nor bays crown
Thy vast desert ; save that, we nothing can
Depute to be thy ashes' guardian.
So jewelers no art or metal trust
To form the diamond, but the diamond's dust.

H. K.[1]

IN OBITUM VENERABILIS VIRI
JOHANNIS DONNE,

sacrae Theologiae Doctoris, Ecclesiae Cathedralis D. Pauli
nuper Decani ; illi honoris, tibi[2] (multum mihi colende Vir)
observantiae ergo haec ego.

1635.

Conquerar? ignavoque sequar tua funera planctu?
Sed lachrymae clausistis iter, nec muta querelas
Lingua potest proferre pias : ignoscite, manes
Defuncti, et tacito sinite indulgere dolori.
Sed scelus est tacuisse : cadant in moesta liturae
Verba. Tuis (docta umbra) tuis haec accipe jussis

1 Henry King, later Bishop of Chichester.
2 Perhaps Donne's son, Dr. John Donne the younger.

Coepta, nec officii contemnens pignora nostri
Aversare tua non dignum laude poetam.
O si Pythagorae non vanum dogma fuisset,
Inque meum a vestro migraret pectore pectus
Musa, repentinos tua nosceret urna furores.
Sed frustra, heu frustra, haec votis puerilibus opto!
Tecum abiit, summoque sedens jam monte Thalia
Ridet anhelantes Parnassi et culmina vates
Desperare jubet.   Verum hac nolente coactos
Scribimus audaces numeros, et flebile carmen
Scribimus (O soli qui te dilexit) habendum.
Siccine perpetuus liventia lumina somnus
Clausit? et immerito merguntur funere virtus
Et pietas et quae poterant fecisse beatum
Caetera, sed nec te poterant servare beatum?
    Quo mihi doctrinam? quorsum impallescere chartis
Nocturnis juvat? et totidem olfecisse lucernas?
Decolor et longos studiis deperdere soles
Ut prius aggredior, longamque accessere famam?
Omnia sed frustra: mihi dum cunctisque minatur
Exitium, crudele et inexorabile fatum.
    Nam post te sperare nihil decet: hoc mihi restat
Ut moriar, tenues fugiatque obscurus in auras
Spiritus. O doctis saltem si cognitus umbris,
Illic te, venerande, iterum, venerande, videbo,
Et dulces audire sonos, et verba diserti
Oris, et aeternas dabitur mihi carpere voces.
Queis ferus infernae tacuisset janitor aulae
Auditis, Nilusque minus strepuisset, Arion
Cederet, et sylvas qui post se traxerat Orpheus,

Eloquio sic ille viros, sic ille movere
Voce feros potuit : quis enim tam barbarus aut tam
Facundis nimis infestus non motus, ut illo
Hortante, et blando victus sermone sileret ?
  Sic oculos, sic ille manus, sic ora ferebat,
Singula sic decuere senem, sic omnia.   Vidi,
Audivi et stupui quoties orator in Aede
Paulina stetit, et mira gravitate levantes
Corda oculosque viros tenuit, dum Nestoris ille
Fudit verba (omni quanto mage dulcia melle !)
Nunc habet attonitos, pandit mysteria plebi
Non concessa prius, nondum intellecta ; revolvunt
Mirantes, tacitique arrectis auribus astant.
  Mutatis mox ille modo formaque loquendi
Tristia pertractat, fatumque et flebile mortis
Tempus, et in cineres redeunt quod corpora primos ;
Tunc gemitum cunctos dare, tunc lugere videres,
Forsitan a lachrymis aliquis non temperat, atque
Ex oculis largum stillat rorem ; aetheris illo
Sic pater audito voluit succumbere turbam,
Affectusque ciere suos, et ponere notae
Vocis ad arbitrium, divinae oracula mentis
Dum narrat, rostrisque potens dominatur in altis.
  Quo feror ? audaci et forsan pietate nocenti
In nimia ignoscas vati, qui vatibus olim
Egregium decus, et tanto excellentior unus
Omnibus, inferior quanto est et pessimus, impar
Laudibus hisce tibi qui nunc facit ista poeta.
Et quo nos canimus ? cur haec tibi sacra ? poetae
Desinite : en fati certus, sibi voce canora

II.—14*

Infcrias praemisit olor, cum Carolus Alba
(Ultima volventem et cygnaea voce loquentem)
Nuper eum turba et magnatum audiret in Aula.
    Tunc rex, tunc proceres, clerus tunc astitit illi
Aula frequens.   Sola nunc in tellure recumbit,
Vermibus esca, pio malint nisi parcere : quidni
Incipiant et amare famem ?   Metuere leones
Sic olim, sacrosque artus violare prophetae
Bellua non ausa est quamquam jejuna, sitimque
Optaret nimis humano satiare cruore.
    At non haec de te sperabimus ; omnia carpit
Praedator vermis ; nec talis contigit illi
Praeda diu ; forsan metrico pede serpet ab inde :
Vescere, et exhausto satia te sanguine.   Jam nos
Adsumus ; et post te cupiet quis vivere ?   Post te
Quis volet, aut poterit ? nam post te vivere mors est.
    Et tamen ingratas ignavi ducimus auras :
Sustinet et tibi lingua Vale, vale dicere : parce
Non festinanti aeternum requiescere turbae.
Ipsa satis properat quae nescit Parca morari,
Nunc urgere colum, trahere atque occare videmus.
Quin rursus, venerande, Vale, vale : ordine nos te
Quo Deus et quo dura volet natura sequemur.
    Depositum interea lapides servate fideles.
Foelices illa queis Aedis parte locari
Qua jacet iste datur.   Forsan lapis inde loquetur,
Parturietque viro plenus testantia luctus
Verba, et carminibus quae Donni suggeret illi
Spiritus, insolitos testari voce calores
Incipiet (non sic Pyrrha jactante calebat) : —

Mole sub hac tegitur quicquid mortale relictum est
De tanto mortale viro.   Qui praefuit Aedi huic,
Formosi pecoris pastor, formosior ipse.
Ite igitur, dignisque illum celebrate loquelis,
Et quae demuntur vitae date tempora famae.

*Indignus tantorum meritorum praeco, virtutum
tuarum cultor religiosissimus,*

DANIEL DARNELLY.

ON THE DEATH OF DOCTOR DONNE.

I CANNOT blame those men that knew thee well,
Yet dare not help the world to ring thy knell
In tuneful elegies; there 's not language known
Fit for thy mention, but 't was first thy own;
The epitaphs thou writst have so bereft
Our tongue of wit there is no fancy left
Enough to weep thee; what henceforth we see
Of art or nature must result from thee.
There may perchance some busy gathering friend
Steal from thy own works, and that, varied, lend,
Which thou bestow'st on others, to thy hearse,
And so thou shalt live still in thy own verse;
He that shall venture farther may commit
A pitied error, show his zeal not wit.
Fate hath done mankind wrong; virtue may aim
Reward of conscience, never can, of fame,

Since her great trumpet 's broke, could only give
Faith to the world, command it to believe.
He then must write, that would define thy parts :
Here lies the best Divinity, all the Arts.

EDW. HYDE.

ON DOCTOR DONNE, BY DR. C. B. OF O.[1]

HE that would write an epitaph for thee,
And do it well, must first begin to be
Such as thou wert ; for none can truly know
Thy worth, thy life, but he that hath lived so.
He must have wit to spare and to hurl down,
Enough to keep the gallants of the town,
He must have learning plenty, both the Laws,
Civil and Common, to judge any cause,
Divinity great store, above the rest,
Not of the last edition but the best,
He must have language, travel, all the arts,
Judgment to use, or else he wants thy parts,
He must have friends the highest, able to do,
Such as Maecenas and Augustus too,
He must have such a sickness, such a death,
Or else his vain descriptions come beneath.
    Who then shall write an epitaph for thee,
He must be dead first, let it alone for me.

[1] Dr. Corbet, Bishop of Oxford.

AN ELEGY UPON THE INCOMPARABLE
DOCTOR DONNE.

ALL is not well when such a one as I
Dare peep abroad and write an elegy;
When smaller stars appear and give their light
Phoebus is gone to bed: were it not night,
And the world witless now that Donne is dead,
You sooner should have broke than seen my head.
Dead did I say? Forgive this injury
I do him and his worth's infinity,
To say he is but dead; I dare aver
It better may be termed a massacre,
Than sleep or death; see how the Muses mourn
Upon their oaten reeds, and from his urn
   Threaten the world with this calamity,
   They shall have ballads, but no poetry.

Language lies speechless, and Divinity
Lost such a trump as even to ecstasy
Could charm the soul, and had an influence
To teach best judgments and please dullest sense.
The Court, the Church, the University,
Lost Chaplain, Dean, and Doctor, all these three.
   It was his merit that his funeral
   Could cause a loss so great and general.

If there be any spirit can answer give
Of such as hence depart to such as live,
Speak,— Doth his body there vermiculate,
Crumble to dust, and feel the claws of Fate ?
Methinks corruption, worms, what else is foul,
Should spare the temple of so fair a soul.
I could believe they do, but that I know
What inconvenience might hereafter grow ;
   Succeeding ages would idolatrize,
   And as his numbers, so his relics prize.

If that philosopher which did avow
The world to be but motes, were living now,
He would affirm that th' atoms of his mould,
Were they in several bodies blended, would
Produce new worlds of travellers, divines,
Of linguists, poets, sith these several lines
In him concentred were, and flowing thence
Might fill again the world's circumference.
I could believe this too, and yet my faith
Not want a precedent ; the phoenix hath
(And such was he) a power to animate
Her ashes, and herself perpetuate.
But, busy soul, thou dost not well to pry
Into these secrets ; grief and jealousy
The more they know the further still advance,
And find no way so safe as ignorance.
Let this suffice thee, that his soul which flew
A pitch of all admired, known but of few,

(Save those of purer mould) is now translated
From Earth to Heaven, and there constellated ;
  For, if each priest of God shine as a star,
  His glory is as his gifts, 'bove others far.

Hen : Valentine.

AN ELEGY UPON DOCTOR DONNE.

Is Donne, great Donne deceased? then England say
Thou hast lost a man where language chose to stay
And show its graceful power.[1] I would not praise
That and his vast wit (which in these vain days
Make many proud) but as they served to unlock
That cabinet his mind, where such a stock
Of knowledge was reposed, as all lament
(Or should) this general cause of discontent.
  And I rejoice I am not so severe
But (as I write a line) to weep a tear
For his decease ; such sad extremities
May make such men as I write elegies.
  And wonder not, for when a general loss
Falls on a nation and they slight the cross,
God hath raised prophets to awaken them
From stupefaction; witness my mild pen,

---

[1] Our Donne is dead ; England should mourn, may say,
  We had a man where language chose to stay
  And show her graceful power.

Not used to upbraid the world, though now it must
Freely and boldly, for the cause is just.

    Dull age, Oh I would spare thee, but th' art worse;
Thou art not only dull, but hast a curse
Of black ingratitude; if not, couldst thou
Part with miraculous Donne, and make no vow,
For thee and thine, successively to pay
A sad remembrance to his dying day?

    Did his youth scatter poetry, wherein
Was all philosophy? was every sin,
Charactered in his Satires, made so foul
That some have feared their shapes, and kept their soul
Freer [1] by reading verse? did he give days,
Past marble monuments, to those whose praise
He would perpetuate?   Did he (I fear
The dull will doubt) these at his twentieth year?

    But, more matured, did his full soul conceive
And in harmonious holy numbers weave
A Crown of sacred sonnets, fit to adorn
A dying martyr's brow, or to be worn
On that blest head of Mary Magdalen
After she wiped Christ's feet, but not till then?
Did he (fit for such penitents as she
And he to use) leave us a Litany
Which all devout men love, and sure it shall,
As times grow better, grow more classical?
Did he write hymns, for piety, for wit,
Equal to those great grave Prudentius writ?
Spake he all languages? knew he all laws?
The grounds and use of physic, but because

1 Safer.

'T was mercenary, waived it ? went to see
The blessed place of Christ's nativity ?
Did he return and preach Him ? preach Him so
As none but he could do ? his hearers know [1]
(Such as were blessed to hear him) this is truth.
Did he confirm thy aged ? convert thy youth ?
Did he these wonders ? and is this dear loss
Mourned by so few ? (few for so great a cross.)
 But sure the silent are ambitious all
To be close mourners at his funeral ;
If not, in common pity they forbear
By repetitions to renew our care ;
Or, knowing, grief conceived, concealed, consumes
Man irreparably (as poisoned fumes
Do waste the brain), make silence a safe way
To enlarge the soul from these walls, mud and clay,
(Materials of this body) to remain
With Donne in Heaven, where no promiscuous pain
Lessens the joy we have, for, with him, all
Are satisfied with joys essentiäl.
 My thoughts, dwell on this joy,[2] and do not call
Grief back, by thinking of his funeral ;
Forget he loved me ; waste not my sad years
(Which haste to David's seventy) filled with fears
And sorrow for his death ; forget his parts,
Which find a living grave in good men's hearts :
And (for my first is daily paid for sin)
Forget to pay my second sigh for him ;

---

1 As since St. Paul none did, none could ? Those know.
2 Dwell on this joy, my thoughts.

Forget his powerful preaching ; and forget
I am his convert.　Oh my frailty! let
My flesh be no more heard, it will obtrude
This lethargy : so should my gratitude,
My vows [1] of gratitude should so be broke ;
Which can no more be, than Donne's virtues spoke
By any but himself, for which cause, I
Write no encomium, but an [2] elegy. [3]

Iz. Wa.

ELEGY ON D. D.

1635.

Now, by one year, time and our frailty have
Lessened our first confusion, since the grave
Closed thy dear ashes, and the tears which flow
In these have no springs but of solid woe ;
Or they are drops which cold amazement froze
At thy decease, and will not thaw in prose.
All streams of verse which shall lament that day,
Do truly to the Ocean tribute pay;
But they have lost their saltness, which the eye,
In recompense of wit, strives to supply.

---

[1] flows.　[2] this.
[3] In the editions subsequent to that of 1633 the following verses are added :
    " Which, as a freewill offering, I here give
    Fame and the world, and parting with it grieve
    I want abilities fit to set forth
    A monument great as Donne's matchless worth."

Passion's excess for thee we need not fear,
Since first by thee our passions hallowed were ;
Thou mad'st our sorrows, which before had bin
Only for the success, sorrows for sin ;
We owe thee all those tears, now thou art dead,
Which we shed not, which for ourselves we shed.
Nor didst thou only consecrate our tears,
Give a religious tincture to our fears,
But even our joys had learned an innocence,
Thou didst from gladness separate offence.
All minds at once sucked grace from thee, as where
(The curse revoked) the nations had one ear.
Pious dissector! thy one hour didst treat
The thousand mazes of the heart's deceit,
Thou didst pursue our loved and subtle sin,
Through all the foldings we had wrapped it in ;
And in thine own large mind finding the way
By which ourselves we from ourselves convey,
Didst in us, narrow models, know the same
Angles, though darker, in our meaner frame.
How short of praise is this ! My Muse, alas,
Climbs weakly to that truth which none can pass ;
He that writes best may only hope to leave
A character of all he could conceive,
But none of thee, and with me must confess
That fancy finds some check from an excess
Of merit most, of nothing it has spun,
And truth, as reason's task and theme, doth shun ;
She makes a fairer flight in emptiness,
Than when a bodied truth doth her oppress.

Reason again denies her scales, because
Hers are but scales, she judges by the laws
Of weak comparison, thy virtue slights
Her feeble beam, and her unequal weights.
What prodigy of wit and piety
Hath she else known, by which to measure thee?
Great soul! we can no more the worthiness
Of what you were, than what you are, express.

SIDNEY GODOLPHIN.

ON DR. JOHN DONNE, LATE DEAN OF SAINT PAUL'S, LONDON.

1635.

LONG since this task of tears from you was due,
Long since, O poets, he did die to you,
Or left you dead when wit and he took flight
On divine wings and soared out of your sight.
Preachers, 't is you must weep; the wit he taught
You do enjoy; the rebels which he brought
From ancient discord, giant faculties,
And now no more religion's enemies;
Honest to knowing, unto virtuous sweet,
Witty to good, and learnèd to discreet,
He reconciled, and bid the usurper go;
Dulness to vice, religion ought to flow;

He kept his loves, but not his objects; wit
He did not banish, but transplanted it,
Taught it his place and use, and brought it home
To piety, which it doth best become;
He showed us how for sins we ought to sigh,
And how to sing Christ's epithalamy;
The altars had his fires, and there he spoke
Incense of love's and fancy's holy smoke:
Religion thus enriched, the people trained,
And God from dull vice had the fashion gained.
The first effects sprung in the giddy mind
Of flashy youth, and thirst of woman-kind
By colors led and drawn to a pursuit
Now once again by beauty of the fruit,
As if their longings too must set us free,
And tempt us now to the commanded tree.
Tell me, had ever pleasure such a dress?
Have you known crimes so shaped? or loveliness
Such as his lips did clothe religion in?
Had not reproof a beauty passing sin?
Corrupted nature sorrowed when she stood
So near the danger of becoming good,
And wished our so inconstant ears exempt
From piety that had such power to tempt.
Did not his sacred flattery beguile
Man to amendment? The law, taught to smile,
Pensioned our vanity, and man grew well
Through the same frailty by the which he fell.
Oh, the sick state of man! health doth not please
Our tastes but in the shape of the disease;

II.—15

Thriftless is charity, coward patience,
Justice is cruel, mercy want of sense.
What means our Nature to bar Virtue place,
If she do come in her own clothes and face?
Is good a pill we dare not chaw to know?
Sense, the soul's servant, doth it keep us so
As we might starve for good, unless it first
Do leave a pawn of relish in the gust?
Or have we to salvatiön no tie
At all but that of our infirmity?
Who treats with us must our affections move
To th' good we fly by those sweets which we love,
Must seek our palates, and with their delight
To gain our deeds must bribe our appetite.
These trains he knew, and laying nets to save,
Temptingly sugared all the health he gave.
But where is now that chime? that harmony
Hath left the world, now the loud organ may
Appear, the better voice is fled to have
A thousand times the sweetness which it gave.
I cannot say how many thousand spirits
The single happiness this soul inherits
Damns in the other world, souls whom no cross
O'th sense afflicts, but only of the loss,
Whom ignorance would half save, all whose pain
Is not in what they feel, but others gain,
Self-executing wretched spirits, who
Carrying their guilt transport their envy too.
But those high joys which his wit's youngest flame,
Would hurt to choose, shall not we hurt to name?

Verse statues are all robbers, all we make
Of monument thus doth not give but take ;
As sails which seamen to a forewind fit
By a resistance go along with it,
So pens grow while they lessen fame so left ;
A weak assistance is a kind of theft.
Who hath not love to ground his tears upon
Must weep here if he have ambitiön.

I. CHUDLEIGH.

AN ELEGY UPON THE DEATH OF THE DEAN OF PAUL'S, DR. JOHN DONNE.

BY MR. THO : CARY.

CAN we not force from widowed Poetry,
Now thou art dead, great Donne, one elegy
To crown thy hearse ? Why yet dare we not trust
Though with unkneaded, dough-baked prose thy dust,
Such as the unscissored churchman from the flower
Of fading rhetoric, short-lived as his hour,
Dry as the sand that measures it, should lay
Upon thy ashes on the funeral day ?
Have we no voice, no tune ? Didst thou dispense
Through all our language both the words and sense ?
'T is a sad truth ; the pulpit may her plain
And sober Christian precepts still retain,

Doctrines it may and wholesome uses frame,
Grave homilies and lectures, but the flame
Of thy brave soul that shot such heat and light
As burnt our earth and made our darkness bright,
Committed holy rapes upon our will,
Did through the eye the melting heart distil,
And the deep knowledge of dark truths so teach,
As sense might judge what fancy could not reach,
Must be desired for ever.   So the fire,
That fills with spirit and heat the Delphic choir,
Which, kindled first by thy Promethean breath,
Glowed here a while, lies quenched now in thy death.
The Muses' garden with pedantic weeds
O'erspread was purged by thee ; the lazy seeds
Of servile imitation thrown away,
And fresh invention planted, thou didst pay
The debts of our penurious bankrupt age ;
Licentious thefts that make poetic rage
A mimic fury, when our souls must be
Possessed or with Anacreon's ecstasy
Or Pindar's not their own ; the subtle cheat
Of sly exchanges, and the juggling feat
Of two-edged words, or whatsoever wrong
By ours was done the Greek or Latin tongue,
Thou hast redeemed, and opened us a mine
Of rich and pregnant fancy, drawn a line
Of masculine expression which had good
Old Orpheus seen, or all the ancient brood
Our superstitious fools admire and hold
Their lead more precious than thy burnished gold,

Thou hadst been their exchequer, and no more
They each in other's dust had raked for ore.
Thou shalt yield no precedence but of time
And the blind fate of language whose tuned chime
More charms the outward sense ; yet thou mayest claim
From so great disadvantage greater fame,
Since to the awe of thy imperious wit,
Our stubborn language bends, made only fit
With her tough, thick-ribbed hoops to gird about
Thy giant fancy, which had proved too stout
For their soft melting phrases.   As in time
They had the start, so did they cull the prime
Buds of invention many a hundred year,
And left the rifled fields, besides the fear
To touch their harvest, yet from those bare lands
Of what is purely thine thy only hands
(And that thy smallest work) have gleanëd more
Than all those times and tongues could reap before.
But thou art gone, and thy strict laws will be
Too hard for libertines in poetry.
They will repeal the goodly exiled train
Of gods and goddesses, which in thy just reign
Were banished nobler poems ; now with these
The silenced tales o' th' Metamorphoses
Shall stuff their lines and swell the windy page,
Till verse, refined by thee in this last age,
Turn ballad rhyme, or those old idols be
Adored again with new apostasy.
Oh, pardon me, that break with untuned verse
The reverend silence that attends thy hearse,

II.—15*

Whose awful solemn murmurs were to thee,
More than these faint lines, a loud elegy,
That did proclaim in a dumb eloquence
The death of all the arts, whose influence
Grown feeble in these panting numbers lies
Gasping short-winded accents, and so dies :
So doth the swiftly turning wheel not stand
In th' instant we withdraw the moving hand,
But some small time maintains a faint weak course
By virtue of the first impulsive force ;
And so whilst I cast on thy funeral pile
Thy crown of bays, oh, let it crack a while
And spit disdain, till the devouring flashes
Suck all the moisture up, then turn to ashes.
I will not draw the envy to engross
All thy perfections, or weep all our loss ;
Those are too numerous for an elegy,
And this too great to be expressed by me.
Though every pen should share a distinct part,
Yet art thou theme enough to tire all Art.
Let others carve the rest, it shall suffice
I on thy tomb this epitaph incise :

Here lies a King that ruled as he thought fit
The universal monarchy of wit ;
Here lie two Flamens and both those the best,
Apollo's first, at last the true God's priest.

AN ELEGY ON DR. DONNE.

BY SIR LUCIUS CARY.

POETS, attend the elegy I sing
Both of a doubly-naméd Priest and King ;
Instead of coats and pennons, bring your verse,
For you must be chief mourners at his hearse ;
A tomb your muse must to his fame supply,
No other monuments can never die.
And as he was a twofold priest, in youth
Apollo's, afterwards the voice of truth,
God's conduit-pipe for grace, who chose him for
His extraordinary ambassador,
So let his liegers with the poets join,
Both having shares, both must in grief combine :
Whilst Jonson forceth with his elegy
Tears from a grief-unknowing Scythian's eye,
Like Moses at whose stroke the waters gushed
From forth the rock and like a torrent rushed,
Let Laud his funeral sermon preach, and show
Those virtues dull eyes were not apt to know,
Nor leave that piercing theme till it appears
To be Good Friday by the church's tears ;
Yet make not grief too long oppress our powers,
Lest that his funeral sermon should prove ours.
Nor yet forget that heavenly eloquence,
With which he did the bread of life dispense,

Preacher and orator discharged both parts,
With pleasure for our sense, health for our hearts,
And the first such (though a long-studied art
Tell us our soul is all in every part),
None was so marble, but whilst him he hears,
His soul so long dwelt only in his ears,
And from thence, with the fierceness of a flood
Bearing down vice, victualled with that blest food
Their hearts ; his seed in none could fail to grow,
Fertile he found them all, or made them so ;
No druggist of the soul bestowed on all
So catholicly a curing cordiäl.
Nor only in the pulpit dwelt his store,
His words worked much, but his example more
That preached on worky days ; his poetry
Itself was oftentimes divinity ;
Those anthems (almost second Psalms) he writ
To make us know the Cross and value it,
(Although we owe that reverence to that name
We should not need warmth from an under-flame)
Create a fire in us so near extreme,
That we would die for and upon this theme :
Next, his so pious Litany which none can
But count divine, except a Puritan,
And that but for the name, nor this nor those
Want anything of sermons but the prose.
Experience makes us see that many a one
Owes to his country his religiön,
And in another would as strongly grow,
Had but his nurse and mother taught him so ;

Not he the ballast on his judgment hung,
Nor did his preconceit do either wrong;
He laboured to exclude whatever sin
By time or carelessness had entered in ;
Winnowed the chaff from wheat, but yet was loth
A too hot zeal should force him burn them both ;
Nor would allow of that so ignorant gall
Which to save blotting often would blot all ;
Nor did those barbarous opinions own,
To think the organs sin, and faction none.
Nor was there expectation to gain grace
From forth his sermons only, but his face,
So primitive a look, such gravity
With humbleness, and both with piety ;
So mild was Moses' countenance when he prayed
For them whose Satanism his power gainsaid,
And such his gravity, when all God's band
Received His word through him at second hand,
Which joined did flames of more devotion move
Than ever Argive Helen's could of love.
Now to conclude, I must my reason bring
Wherefore I called him in his title king ;
That kingdom the philosophers believed
To excel Alexander's, nor were grieved
By fear of loss (that being such a prey
No stronger than one's self can force away),
The kingdom of one's self, this he enjoyed,
And his authority so well employed,
That never any could before become
So great a monarch in so small a room.

He conquered rebel passions, ruled them so,
As under-spheres by the first mover go ;
Banished so far their working that we can
But know he had some, for we knew him man.
Then let his last excuse his first extremes,
His age saw visions, though his youth dreamed dreams.

ON DR. DONNE'S DEATH: BY MR. MAYNE OF CHRIST-CHURCH IN OXFORD.

WHO shall presume to mourn thee, Donne, unless
He could his tears in thy expressions dress,
And teach his grief, that reverence of thy hearse,
To weep lines learnèd as thy Anniverse ?
A poem of that worth, whose every tear
Deserves the title of a several year ;
Indeed so far above its reader, good,
That we are thought wits when 't is understood ;
There that blest maid to die, who now should grieve ?
After thy sorrow, 't were her loss to live,
And her fair virtues in another's line,
Would faintly dawn, which are made saints in thine.
Hadst thou been shallower, and not writ so high,
Or left some new way for our pen or eye
To shed a funeral tear, perchance thy tomb
Had not been speechless or our Muses dumb ;

But now we dare not write, but must conceal
Thy epitaph, lest we be thought to steal;
For who hath read thee and discerns thy worth
That will not say thy careless hours brought forth
Fancies beyond our studies, and thy play
Was happier than our serious time of day?
So learnèd was thy chance thy haste had wit,
And matter from thy pen flowed rashly fit;
What was thy recreation turns our brain,
Our rack and paleness is thy weakest strain,
And when we most come near thee, 't is our bliss
To imitate thee where thou dost amiss.
Here light your muse, you that do only think
And write, and are just poets as you drink,
In whose weak fancies wit doth ebb and flow
Just as your reckonings rise, that we may know
In your whole carriage of your work, that here
This flash you wrote in wine, and that in beer;
This is to tap your muse, which, running long,
Writes flat, and takes our ear not half so strong;
Poor suburb wits, who, if you want your cup,
Or if a Lord recover, are blown up;
Could you but reach this height, you should not need
To make, each meal, a project ere you feed,
Nor walk in relics, clothes so old and bare
As if left off to you from Ennius were,
Nor should your love in verse call mistress those
Who are mine hostess or your whores in prose;
From this muse learn to court, whose power could move
A cloistered coldness or a vestal love,

And would convey such errands to their ear,
That ladies knew no odds to grant and hear.
But I do wrong thee, Donne, and this low praise
Is written only for thy younger days;
I am not grown up for thy riper parts,
Then should I praise thee through the tongues and arts,
And have that deep divinity to know
What mysteries did from thy preaching flow,
Who with thy words could charm thy audience,
That at thy sermons ear was all our sense;
Yet have I seen thee in the pulpit stand,
Where we might take notes from thy look and hand,
And from thy speaking action bear away
More sermon that some teachers used to say.
Such was thy carriage, and thy gesture such,
As could divide the heart, and conscience touch;
Thy motion did confute, and we might see
An error vanquished by delivery.
Not like our Sons of Zeal, who, to reform
Their hearers, fiercely at the pulpit storm,
And beat the cushion into worse estate
Than if they did conclude it reprobate,
Who can out-pray the glass, then lay about
Till all predestination be run out,
And from the point such tedious uses draw,
Their repetitions would make Gospel, Law.
No, in such temper would thy sermons flow,
So well did doctrine and thy language show,
And had that holy fear, as, hearing thee,
The Court would mend and a good Christian be,

And ladies though unhandsome, out of grace,
Would hear thee in their unbought looks and face.
More I could write, but let this crown thine urn,—
We cannot hope the like till thou return.

UPON MR. J. DONNE AND HIS POEMS.

Who dares say thou art dead, when he doth see
Unburied yet this living part of thee?
This part that to thy being gives fresh flame,
And though thou 'rt Donne, yet will preserve thy name.
Thy flesh, whose channels left their crimson hue
And whey-like ran at last in a pale blue,
May show thee mortal, a dead palsy may
Seize on 't and quickly turn it into clay,
Which like the Indian earth shall rise refined,
But this great spirit thou hast left behind,
This soul of verse in its first pure estate,
Shall live for all the world to imitate
But not come near, for in thy fancy's flight
Thou dost not stoop unto the vulgar sight,
But hovering highly in the air of wit
Holdst such a pitch that few can follow it,
Admire they may.   Each object that the Spring
Or a more piercing influence doth bring
To adorn earth's face, thou sweetly didst contrive
To beauty's elements, and thence derive

Unspotted lilies white which thou didst set
Hand in hand with the vein-like violet,
Making them soft and warm, and by thy power
Couldst give both life and sense unto a flower.
The cherries thou hast made to speak will be
Sweeter unto the taste than from the tree,
And, spite of winter storms, amidst the snow
Thou oft hast made the blushing rose to grow.
The sea-nymphs that the watery caverns keep
Have sent their pearls and rubies from the deep
To deck thy love, and placed by thee they drew
More lustre to them than where first they grew.
All minerals, that earth's full womb doth hold
Promiscuously, thou couldst convert to gold,
And with thy flaming raptures so refine
That it was much more pure than in the mine.
The lights that gild the night, if thou didst say
They look like eyes, those did outshine the day;
For there would be more virtue in such spells
Than in meridians or cross parallels;
Whatever was of worth in this great frame,
That art could comprehend or wit could name,
It was thy theme for beauty; thou didst see
Woman was this fair world's epitome.
Thy nimble satires too, and every strain
With nervy strength that issued from thy brain,
Will lose the glory of their own clear bays
If they admit of any other praise.
But thy diviner poems, whose clear fire
Purges all dross away, shall by a choir

Of cherubims with heavenly notes be set,
Where flesh and blood could ne'er attain to yet;
There purest spirits sing such sacred lays
In panegyric hallelujaës.

ARTHUR WILSON.

IN MEMORY OF DR. DONNE.

BY MR. R. B.

DONNE dead? 'T is here reported true, though I
Ne'er yet so much desired to hear a lie;
'T is too too true, for so we find it still,
Good news are often false, but seldom, ill:
But must poor fame tell us his fatal day,
And shall we know his death the common way?
Methinks some comet bright should have foretold
The death of such a man, for though of old
'T is held that comets princes' death foretell,
Why should not his have needed one as well
Who was the prince of wits, 'mongst whom he reigned
High as a prince, and as great state maintained?
Yet wants he not his sign, for we have seen
A dearth, the like to which hath never been,
Treading on harvest's heels, which doth presage
The dearth of wit and learning which this age
Shall find now he is gone; for though there be
Much grain in show, none brought it forth as he;

Or men are misers, or if true want raises
The dearth, then more that dearth Donne's plenty praises.
Of learning, languages, of eloquence,
And poesie, past ravishing of sense,
He had a magazine wherein such store
Was laid up as might hundreds serve of poor.
   But he is gone, oh, how will his desire
Torture all those that warmed them by his fire ?
Methinks I see him in the pulpit standing,
Not ears or eyes, but all men's hearts commanding,
Where we that heard him to ourselves did fain
Golden Chrysostome was alive again ;
And never were we wearied till we saw
His hour, and but an hour, to end did draw.
How did he shame the doctrine-men, and use,
With helps to boot, for men to bear th' abuse
Of their tired patience, and endure th' expense
Of time, oh spent in hearkening to non-sense,
With marks also enough whereby to know
The speaker is a zealous dunce or so.
'T is true they quitted him, to their poor power
They hummed against him, and with face most sour
Called him a strong-lined man, a macaroon,
And no way fit to speak to clouted shoon,
As fine words truly as you would desire
But verily but a bad edifier.
Thus did these beetles slight in him that good
They could not see, and much less, understood.
But we may say when we compare the stuff
Both brought : he was a candle, they the snuff.

Well, Wisdom 's of her children justified,
Let therefore these poor fellows stand aside ;
Nor, though of learning he deserved so highly,
Would I his book should save him; rather slily
I should advise his clergy not to pray,
Though of the learnedst sort ; methinks that they
Of the same trade are judges not so fit,
There 's no such emulation as of wit ;
Of such, the envy might as much perchance
Wrong him, and more, than th' others' ignorance.
It was his fate (I know 't) to be envíed
As much by clerks, as laymen magnified ;
And why ? but 'cause he came late in the day,
And yet his penny earned, and had, as they.
No more of this lest some should say that I
Am strayed to satire, meaning elegy.
No, no, had Donne need to be judged or tried,
A jury I would summon on his side
That had no sides nor factions, past the touch
Of all exceptions, freed from passion, such
As not to fear nor flatter e'er were bred,
These would I bring though callëd from the dead :
Southampton, Hamilton, Pembroke, Dorset's earls,
Huntingdon, Bedford's countesses — the pearls
Once of each sex.   If these suffice not, I
Ten *decem tales* have of standers-by :
All which, for Donne, would such a verdict give
As can belong to none that now doth live.
　　But what do I ?   A diminution 't is
To speak of him in verse so short of his,'

II.—16

Whereof he was the master.   All indeed
Compared with him piped on an oaten reed :
Oh that you had but one 'mongst all your brothers
Could write for him as he hath done for others !
Poets I speak to.   When I see 't I 'll say
My eyesight betters as my years [1] decay ;
Meantime a quarrel I shall ever have   ,
Against these doughty keepers from the grave,
Who use, it seems, their old authority
When, Verses men immortal make, they cry;
Which had it been a recipe true tried,
Probatum esset, Donne had never died.
    For me, if e'er I had least spark at all
Of that which they poetic fire do call,
Here I confess it fetchëd from his hearth
Which is gone out now he is gone to earth.
This only a poor flash, a lightning is
Before my muse's death, as after his.
Farewell, fair soul, and deign receive from me
This type of that devotion I owe thee,
From whom while living as by voice and pen
I learned more than from a thousand men,
So by thy death, am of one doubt released,
And now believe that miracles are ceased.

[1] ears, 1649, '54, '69.

EPITAPH UPON DR. DONNE.

BY ENDYMION PORTER.

This decent urn a sad inscription wears
Of Donne's departure from us to the spheres;
And the dumb stone with silence seems to tell
The changes of this life, wherein is well
Expressed a cause to make all joy to cease
And never let our sorrows more take ease;
For now it is impossible to find
One fraught with virtues to enrich a mind.
But why should death with a promiscuous hand
At one rude stroke impoverish a land?
Thou strict attorney unto stricter Fate
Didst thou confiscate his life out of hate
To his rare parts? Or didst thou throw thy dart
With envious hand at some plebeian heart,
And he with pious virtue stepped between
To save that stroke, and so was killed unseen
By thee? Oh, 't was his goodness so to do,
Which human kindness never reached unto.
Thus the hard laws of death were satisfied,
And he left us like orphan friends and died.
Now from the pulpit to the people's ears
Whose speech shall send repentant sighs and tears?
Or tell me, if a purer virgin die,
Who shall hereafter write her elegy?

Poets, be silent, let your numbers sleep,
For he is gone that did all fancy keep;
Time hath no soul but his exalted verse,
Which with amazements we may now rehearse.

EPITAPH.

Here lies Dean Donne.   Enough : those words alone
Show him as fully as if all the stone
His Church of Paul's contains were through inscribed,
Or all the walkers there, to speak him, bribed.
None can mistake him, for one such as he
Donne, Dean, or man, more none shall ever see.
Not man?   No, though unto a sun each eye
Were turned, the whole earth so to overspy.
A bold, brave word; yet such brave spirits as knew
His spirit, will say it is less bold than true.

NOTES.

NOTES.

Page 3.

To Mr. Christopher Brooke.

Christopher Brooke was one of Donne's early and intimate friends, and his chamber-fellow in Lincoln's Inn, to which Donne was admitted when nineteen years old, in 1592. There, says Anthony à Wood, Brooke "became known to and admired by Joh. Selden, Ben Jonson, Mich. Drayton, Will Browne, George Withers, and Joh. Davies of Hereford." (*Fasti Oxon.* ed. Bliss, i, 403.) He was himself a writer of verse which was admired, or at least highly eulogized, by some of his contemporaries. When Donne was secretly married in 1600, Brooke gave him his wife and witnessed his marriage, and for so doing was, at the instance of Sir George More, the father of Donne's wife, committed for a time to prison, as was also his brother, the Rev. Samuel Brooke, who had performed the marriage, as well as Donne himself.

Page 3.

The Storm and *The Calm.*

These letters describe incidents of what was called the Island Voyage, an expedition in 1597 under the Earl of Essex, with the intent of intercepting and capturing the Spanish treasure-fleet on its return from the West Indies, at the Azores, where it was expected to touch. The expedition was on a great scale, and attracted many gentleman-volunteers, of whom Donne was one. It set sail from Plymouth on the 5th of July, but had not proceeded more than forty leagues when it met with a violent storm. Essex contended against the gale till his ship was near sinking. His own graphic account of the storm reports that the main- and fore-masts of his vessel were cracked, her beams broken and reft, and her seams opened. (*Harl. MSS.* 36, 419, cited in *Lives and Letters of Devereux, Earls of Essex.* By the Hon. W. B. Devereux, London, 1853, i, 431.) Many of the vessels were wholly disabled, and the shattered fleet was obliged to return in great confusion and distress to Plymouth in order to refit. Many of the gentleman-volunteers had had enough of the sea, and were glad to stay at home. Donne seems to have stuck by his ship, and to have accompanied the diminished squadron when it set out again for the islands. The expedition failed in its main object, and returned to England in October.

Page 3.

" Thou, which art I ('t is nothing to be so)."

Dr. Grosart, whose lack of perspicacity is sometimes as amusing as his carelessness is annoying, prints this verse as follows:

" Thou which art ! ('t is nothing to be soe)."

Page 3.

"By Hilliard drawn."

Nicholas Hilliard (1547–1619) was limner, jeweler, and goldsmith to Queen Elizabeth and afterward to King James. He painted delicately in miniature, with curious detail, and his work was much admired and prized, but it lacked force and truth to nature. See Walpole's *Anecdotes of Painting in England,* edited by Wornum, i, 171, where is an engraving of Hilliard's miniature of himself.

Page 3.

. . . "a wind,
Which at th' air's middle marble room did find
Such strong resistance that itself it threw
Downward again."

Blundeville, in *His Exercises,* London, 1594, p. 179, says : "This element [the air] is divided of the natural Philosophers into three Regions, that is to say, the highest Region, the middle Region, and the lowest Region. . . . The middle Region is extreme cold."

Bacon, in his *Historia Ventorum*, says : "Since the cold in the middle region of the air is plainly very intense, it is evident that vapours cannot for the most part penetrate those regions, but must be either congealed or hurled back again. And this was the opinion of the ancients, which in this instance is sound." Headlam's translation, in Spedding's *Works of Bacon*, v, 163.

Page 5.

"Compared to these storms, death is but a qualm,
Hell somewhat lightsome, and the Bermuda calm."

"For the Islands of the Bermudas, as every man knoweth that hath heard or read of them, were . . . ever esteemed and reputed a most prodigious and enchanted place, affording nothing but gusts, stormes and foule weather." *A Discovery of Bermudas, otherwise called the Ile of Divils*, by Sil. Jourdan, London, 1610. In Goldsmid's *Hakluyt* (1890), xv, 185.

See also Furness's edition of *The Tempest*, note on "still-vext *Bermoothes*," act i, sc. 2, 269, and *Appendix*, pp. 276 sqq.

Page 6.

. . . "as the isles which we

Seek."

These words determine the voyage to which *The Storm* and *The Calm* relate.

Page 7.

"Earth's hollownesses, which the world's lungs are."

It was a common belief that winds were breathed out of the earth. One of the articles of inquiry in Bacon's *Historia Ventorum* is, concerning the winds "which breathe forth from the hollows of the earth, whether they rush out in a body or exhale imperceptibly."

Page 7.

"Only the calenture together draws
Dear friends, which meet dead in great fishes' jaws."

Calenture, "a name formerly given to a furious delirium, accompanied by fever, which sometimes led the affected person to imagine the sea to be a green field and to throw himself into it."

Page 7.

"Now as a myriad
Of ants durst th' emperor's loved snake invade."

The emperor was Tiberius. "Erat ci in oblectamentis serpens draco, quem ex consuetudine manu sua cibaturus, cum consumptum a formicis invenisset, monitus est ut vim multitudinis caveret."

Suetonius, Tib. 72.

Page 8.

To Sir Henry Wotton.

Wotton was an early and lifelong friend of Donne. Betwixt them, says Walton, "there was so mutual a knowledge, and such a friendship contracted in their youth, as nothing but death could force a separation." Wotton was five years the elder, and he survived Donne by eight years.

Wotton went on the Island Voyage, and it was possibly his going that induced Donne to undertake it.

Page 8.

"To a bottle of hay."

"Methinks I have a great desire to a bottle of hay," says Bottom (*M. N. D.*, iv, 1, 37). "Bottle" in this sense of bundle has dropped out of use. It was from the old French *botteau*.

Page 8.

"Remoras," see note on p. 116, Vol. I.

Page 10.

" Only in this one thing be no Galenist."

One of the fundamental maxims of Galen was, that disease is something contrary to nature, and is to be overcome by a remedy contrary to the disease itself.

In the next verse, for "court's" read "courts'."

Page 11.

" Having from these sucked all they had of worth."

According to Walton, in his *Life of Wotton*, Sir Henry, after leaving Oxford, spent almost nine years on the Continent.

Page 11.

To Sir Henry Goodyere.

Sir Henry Goodyere (or Goodere) appears to have been one of Donne's most faithful friends. He was of the circle of wits and courtiers which surrounded the Countess of Bedford. Two of Ben Jonson's Epigrams are addressed to him, the second of which begins :

" When I would know thee, Goodyere, my thought looks
Upon thy well-made choice of friends and books."

He was knighted by Queen Elizabeth in 1599, and was much about the court. He took part in the performance of Ben Jonson's *Barriers*, at the celebration of the ill-starred marriage of the Earl of Essex and Lady Frances Howard in 1606. He had a fine seat at Polesworth in Warwickshire, to which Burton refers in *The Anatomy of Melancholy*, Part 2, Sect. 2, Member 3.

Page 13.

" And tables or fruit-trenchers teach as much."

"Tables" were small, portable memorandum-books. Douce, in his *Illustrations of Shakspeare*, London, 1807, says : "It is remarkable that neither public nor private museums should furnish any specimens of these table-books, which seem to have been very common in the time of Shakspeare." "They were sometimes made of slate with leaves and clasps." (ii, 227.) Fruit-trenchers, or trenchers of other use, were customarily adorned with moral maxims or posies. "I 'll have you make twelve posies for a dozen of cheese-trenchers," says one of the characters in Webster's *Northward Ho.*

Page 13.

"You came with me to Micham, and are here."

From 1606 to 1611 Donne lived at Mitcham, in Surrey, a few miles south of London. His fortunes were low, his prospects uncertain, his health infirm. It was while he was in this retirement that he wrote many, perhaps most, of his poetical *Epistles*, and many of the *Letters* which were printed in 1651. He was wearing out his heart in hope of court favor and preferment. He had become a favorite with the king. He was urged to take orders in the church, but relucted against doing so, hoping for employment in affairs, like his friend Wotton. He was an assiduous flatterer of those who might befriend him. But at the same time he was reading widely and deeply, and becoming no less a scholar than poet, and as poet there was none at court to compare with him.

Page 13.

To Mr. Rowland Woodward.

Of Mr. Rowland Woodward I know nothing. Dr. Bliss, in a note in his edition of Anthony à Wood's *Athenæ Oxonienses*, iii, 255, mentions a letter by Row. Woodward, relating to the Spanish match, reprinted by Gutch in the first volume of his *Collectanea Curiosa*, 1781.

Page 15.

To Sir Henry Wotton.

. . . "I may as well
Tell you Calais' or Saint Michael's tale for news "—
That is, tales of the old wars with France.

Page 16.

To the Countess of Bedford.

Lucy Harington, the Countess of Bedford, the patroness of poets, sung by Daniel and Jonson and many another, as well as by Donne. Greatly renowned in her own time, she is famous now and always through Jonson's noble epigram, which I cannot forbear citing in full, not only for its own sake, but because of the justification it affords of the eulogy in Donne's verses.

ON LUCY, COUNTESS OF BEDFORD.

This morning, timely wrapped with holy fire,
    I thought to form unto my zealous Muse,
What kind of creature I could most desire,
    To honour, serve, and love ; as poets use.
I meant to make her fair and free and wise,
    Of greatest blood, and yet more good than great ;
I meant the day-star should not brighter rise,
    Nor lend like influence from his lucent seat ;
I meant she should be courteous, facile, sweet,
    Hating that solemn vice of greatness, pride ;
I meant each softest virtue there should meet,
    Fit in that softer bosom to reside.
Only a learnëd and a manly soul
    I purposed her ; that should, with even powers,
The rock, the spindle, and the sheers control
    Of Destiny, and spin her own free hours.
Such when I meant to feign, and wished to see,
My Muse bade, Bedford write, and that was she !

Page 19.

To the Countess of Bedford.

        "And after this survey oppose to all
            Babblers of chapels, you, th' Escurial."

You surpass other women as the Escurial —"unica maravilla del mundo "— surpasses all other sacred edifices.

Page 21.

To Sir Edward Herbert, at Juliers.

Sir Edward Herbert, better known as Lord Herbert of Cherbury, gives an account of his exploits at the siege of Juliers in 1610, in his Life of himself, London, 1792, page 74 sqq. This book is one of the most remarkable and entertaining autobiographies in English, displaying in Lord Herbert one of the belated, romantic spirits of the Renaissance.

Page 22.

' "Thus man, that might be his pleasure, is his rod."
"His"—his own.

Page 25.

To the Countess of Bedford.

"We have . . . sent
Two new stars lately to the firmament."

These two new stars were Prince Henry, who died November 6, 1612, and the brother of the Countess, Lord Harington, who died early in 1613.

Page 29.

To the Countess of Huntingdon.

Lady Elizabeth Stanley, daughter of the Earl of Derby. She was married in 1603 to Henry Hastings, fifth Earl of Huntingdon, and died in 1633.

In a letter of Donne's to Sir Henry Goodyere, undated, but written, as its contents show, in 1626, he says: "I reserve not the mention of my Lady Huntingdon to the end of my Letter as grains to make the gold weight, but as tincture to make the better gold. . . . I beseech you let her Ladyship know that she hath sowed her favours to me in such a ground, that if I be grown better (as I hope I am) her favours are grown with me, and though they were great when she conferred them, yet (if I mend every day) they increase in me every day, and therefore every day multiply my thankfulness towards her Ladyship. Say what you will (if you like not this expression) that may make her Ladyship know, that I shall never let fall the memory nor the just valuation of her noble favours to me, nor leave them unrequited in my exchequer, which is the blessing of God upon my prayers." *Letters*, p. 236.

Page 29.

"Canons will not church-functions you invade."

The meaning of this violent ellipsis is — The canons of the church will not allow you to invade — that is, to assume — church functions.

Page 31.

Stanza II.

The construction of these four verses is unusually perplexed. They may be paraphrased as follows : Inasmuch as all virtues flow from you, and it is even a virtue to dare to contemplate you, I, who venture to do so, owe you tribute for this, and pay it to you in these lines.

Page 32.

To Mr. I. W.

In a copy of the 1633 edition of Donne's poems, with notes by a contemporary hand, which some time since was in Mr. Quaritch's possession, the title at the head of these verses is written out : " To M. I. Walton, perhaps." But Walton had printed few, if any, verses before Donne's death, and the eulogy, in view of Walton's scanty ability as a verse-writer, passes the bounds even of a courtier's flattery. But there is no I. W., known as a poet, to whom they seem appropriate.

Page 33.

To Mr. T. W.

The initials do not reveal the name of this unknown friend of Donne's youth.

Page 35.

To Mr. C. B.

The initials stand for Christopher Brooke, and the S. B. to whom the next poem is addressed was doubtless his brother Samuel.

Page 37.

To Mr. B. B.

These initials, and those which precede the poems on pages 39 and 40, belonged to friends of Donne as yet undetermined. The character of the poems suggests that the I. L. to whom the poem on page 39 is addressed is the same person as the I. P. to whom the next poem is inscribed, and that the L. or the P. is a printer's error.

Page 38.

To Mr. R. W.

R. W. is probably the Rowland Woodward to whom the poem on p. 13 is addressed.

"Never did Morpheus, nor his brother, wear
Shapes so like those shapes whom they would appear."

Donne has in mind Ovid's description of Morpheus and his brother:

. . . "Non illo quisquam sollertius alter
Exprimit incessus, vultumque, sonumque loquendi ;
Adjicit et vestes, et consuetissima cuique
Verba. Sed hic solos homines imitatur. At alter
Fit fera, fit volucris, fit longo corpore serpens.
Hunc Icelon superi, mortale Phobetora vulgus
Nominat." *Metam.* xi, 635–641.

Page 38.

"Guiana's harvest is nipped in the spring."

The disappointments concerning Guiana were many, from Raleigh's first expedition in 1595 to his last in 1618.

Page 41.

To the E. of D.

James Hay, Earl of Doncaster (previously Baron Hay, and afterward Earl of Carlisle) was a Scotch gentleman who came to England with King James, and was one of his favorites, and one of the most splendid noblemen at the court. Clarendon draws a striking portrait of him, — of his universal understanding, his jovial life,

his extravagance, the notable gracefulness and affability of his be-
havior. (*History of the Rebellion*, 1819, i, 112.) In 1619 Donne
accompanied the Earl of Doncaster, as his chaplain, on his ineffectual
embassy to the Emperor on the affairs of the Palatinate. His extravagant expenditure on this errand was such that "the King was
almost ashamed to tell the Parliament how much money the Vis-
count Doncaster's journey cost." "He had with him a great many
noblemen's sons and other persons of quality." Arthur Wilson, in
Kennett's *History of England*, ii, 730.

Two short letters of his to Donne, and one of Donne's to him, show-
ing much friendliness on Doncaster's part, and some servility on
Donne's, are printed in Sir Tobie Mathew's *Collection of Letters* (edited by John Donne, Jr.), London, 1660, pp. 313, 321, 323.

The *Holy Sonnets* sent to the Earl were probably those printed in
this volume, pp. 143-146.

Page 42.

To Sir H. W., at his going Ambassador to Venice.

Wotton was sent as ambassador to Venice in 1604.

Page 46.

To the Countess of Bedford.

"And those are barren both above our head."

The two elements above our head—the air and the fire (according
to the doctrine of the middle ages) — are both barren.

Page 47.

"But as our souls of growth and souls of sense
Have birthright of our reason's soul."

The *anima vegetativa* and the *anima sensitiva* were supposed to
have existence before the *anima intellectiva* was breathed into the
human being. The same medieval doctrine is the motive of a con-
ceit in the poem addressed by Donne to the Countess of Salisbury
(see p. 61).

II.—17

Page 48.

To the Countess of Huntingdon.

This poem, in which are many noble verses, and many obscure, begins with a difficult passage which may be paraphrased as follows: The New World shows us men who would be as naked as Adam before his fall, were it not that they know and fear the wild beasts, and therefore clothe themselves for protection ; and thus they bear the burden of Adam's sin, though they know nothing of the redemption.

Page 50.

"So passion is to woman's love."

The meaning seems to be : Passion is not the true way to love — nay, it rather interferes with progress to genuine love.

Page 51.

"For what is more doth what you are restrain."

What is beyond the truth concerning you, no less than what falls short of it, misses and limits what you are, and in going beyond, instead of staying at the summit of truth, goes down, as it were, on the other side.

Page 51.

"Each good in you 's a light ; so, many a shade
You make, and in them are your motions made."

In the shadows, which are cast by the objects on which your light falls, we move, faintly reflecting back, by our good, the light that streams from you.

Page 52.

"Where thoughts the stars of soul we understand,
We guess not their large natures, but command."

The meaning is obscure, but possibly it may be, where we understand the thoughts, which are to the soul as the stars are to heaven, we do not comprehend their full meaning, their entire nature, but we recognize and admit their authority.

Page 53.

A Dialogue between Sir Henry Wotton and Mr. Donne.

The stanzas of this poem are not to be assigned with certainty to their respective authors, but probably the first three are Wotton's, the last three Donne's.

Page 56.

A Letter to the Lady Carey, and Mrs. Essex Riche, from Amiens.

These ladies were the reputed daughters of Robert, Lord Rich, by Penelope, daughter of Walter Devereux, first Earl of Essex. The divorce of their mother in 1605 was hardly less scandalous than that of the Countess of Essex, their cousin's wife, in 1613. After many years of marriage, during which she had borne five children, Lady Rich abandoned her husband, taking her children with her, declaring them to be the issue of Charles Blount, Earl of Devonshire. The earl received her; her divorce immediately followed, and he married her on the 26th December, 1605. Laud, then a young man, and domestic chaplain of the earl, performed the marriage ceremony, for which he was severely condemned and fell under the displeasure of the king. The earl lived but for a few months after the marriage. "And happy had he been," wrote Mr. Chamberlaine to Secretary Winwood, April 5, 1606, "if he had gone two or three years since, before the world was weary of him, or that he had left that scandal behind him." He was but forty-three years old. See Lodge's *Portraits of Illustrious Personages*, London, 1825, Vol. IV, No. 4.

Page 59.

To the Countess of Salisbury.

Lady Catherine Howard, youngest daughter of Thomas, Earl of Suffolk, and of his beautiful and "rapacious" Countess. She married in 1608 William Cecil, second Earl of Salisbury, grandson of Queen Elizabeth's High Treasurer, Lord Burleigh. The notorious Lady Frances Howard (the Countess of Essex and then of Somerset), who inherited her mother's beauty, was her sister. Donne was flatterer in ordinary of the family. This *Epistle* was written a few months after the *Epithalamium* which celebrated Lady Frances's marriage to Somerset.

Page 61.

. . . "You do
Illustrate them who come to study you"—
"Illustrate" in the sense of "illuminate."

Page 62.

To the Lady Bedford.

Who the lady was whose death is the subject of this poem is uncertain; possibly she was the Countess of Bedford's cousin, Bridget,
Lady Markham, who died in 1609, and on whom Donne composed
the *Elegy* found in this volume, p. 127. On her monument in Twickenham church (the house of the Countess was at Twickenham) is a
remarkable epitaph in which are the following words: "inclytae
Luciae Comitissae de Bedford sanguine (quod satis) sed et amicitiâ
propinquissima." See Lodge's *Portraits*, 1826, V, 9.

Page 62.

"Twins, though their birth Cusco and Musce take."

Twins, though one be born at Cuzco, in Peru, and one at Moscow.

Page 63.

"Yet, but of Judith, no such book as she."

No book, but that of Judith, depicts a woman such as she. Of Judith it is written: "She was of a goodly countenance and very beautiful to behold, and there was none that gave her an ill word," and
"she increased more and more in honour." *Judith*, chs. viii, xvi.

Page 64.

Sappho to Philænis.

Philænis was a poetess of Leucas, of uncertain date, to whom was
ascribed an erotic poem, which, however, is said to have been attrib-
uted to her for the sake of calumniating her. (See *Athenaeus*, viii,
13.) There seems to be no classical authority for connecting her
with Sappho. The fact that her birthplace was near the Leucadian
promontory, from which Sappho took her fatal leap, may have sug-
gested to Donne the association of their names.

Page 67.

To Sir Thomas Rowe, 1603.

The date given to this poem, if correct, makes its interpretation difficult. Donne was married in 1600. But it is better to assume that the date is wrong, and that it was written before his marriage.

I suspect, also, that some verses have been lost after the fourth. As the verses now stand the "Tell her" of the first verse has no proper sequence.

Rowe, or more properly Roe, to whom the verses are addressed, was not knighted till 1604. The year of his birth is uncertain, but he was a somewhat younger contemporary of Donne. He is remembered mainly by his famous embassy in 1614 to the Great Mogul.

Page 71.

An Anatomy of the World.

This poem was first printed, apparently immediately after its composition, in 1611, in 8vo, 16 leaves. In 1612 it was issued, together with *The Progress of the Soul,* each with a separate title-page, — that of *An Anatomy* headed with the words *The first Anniversarie,* and that of *The Progress* with *The second Anniversarie.* Other editions were printed in 1621 and 1625. All of them are without the author's name. They are of extreme rarity.

The verses prefixed to *An Anatomy of the World* are presumably by the same writer as those prefixed to *The Progress of the Soul,* p. 93, entitled "The Harbinger to the Progress," which Jonson told Drummond were by Joseph Hall. (*Conversations,* p. 36.) Hall was already in 1610 eminent as wit, poet, scholar, and divine. He was made bishop of Exeter in 1627.

An Anatomy of the World and *The Progress of the Soul,* the most elaborate of Donne's poems, and the richest in thought and in imagination, were written in honor of a girl whom he had never seen, and who died when she was not fifteen years old. In a letter from Paris, written in November, 1611, to Sir H. Goodyere, Donne says : "I hear from England of many censures of my book of Mistress Drury. If any of those censures do but pardon me my descent of printing anything in verse (which if they do, they are more charitable than myself, for I do not pardon myself, but confess that I did it against my conscience, that is, against my own opinion that I should not have done so), I doubt not but that they will soon give over that other part of the indictment, which is that I have said so much; for nobody can imagine that I, who never saw her, could have any other purpose in that, than that, when I had received so very good testimony of her worthiness, and was gone down to print verses, it became me to say, not what I was sure was just truth, but the best that I could conceive; for that had been a new weakness in me, to have praised anybody in printed verses, that had not been capable of the best praise that I could give." *Letters*, p. 74. Cf. a letter of April 14, 1612, from Paris to G. G[errard, or Garrat], Esquire, *Id.*, p. 238.

Among the censurers of his poem Donne may have reckoned Ben Jonson, whom Drummond reports as saying "that Donne's *Anniversarie* was profane and full of blasphemies; that he told Mr. Donne, if it had been written of the Virgin Mary it had been something; to which he answered that he described the Idea of a Woman, and not as she was." *Conversations*, p. 3.

The excuse for having said "so much" concerning a girl whom he had never seen, is hardly less forced than the extravagance of the eulogy which required it. There was another purpose in his verse than that which he assigns to it. Sir Robert Drury was one of the richest men in England, and Donne was in such straitened circumstances that he may be partly excused for writing with mercenary ends in view. Sir Robert, "a gentleman," says Walton, "of a very noble estate, and a more liberal mind, assigned him [Donne] and his wife a useful apartment in his own large house in Drury Lane, and not only rent free, but was also a cherisher of his studies, and such a friend as sympathized with him and his in all their joys and sorrows." In 1611 Donne was taken by Sir Robert Drury, as his private chaplain, on his complimentary mission to attend the coronation of the Emperor Matthias at Frankfort. They were absent for nine months, and after their return Donne continued to reside at Drury House, where he probably remained till Sir Robert's death in 1615.

Page 79.

. . . "yet when he did depart
With her whom we lament, he lost his heart."

"Depart with"—part with, resign; as in *Love's Labour 's Lost.*
ii, 1, 147:
"Which we much rather had depart withal."

Page 80.

"And new philosophy calls all in doubt ;
The element of fire is quite put out."

These verses and the five following are of interest in their reference
to the new doctrines which the discoveries of Copernicus, Galileo, and
Kepler were introducing.

The old notion of a sphere of fire encompassing that of the air pre-
vailed down to Donne's time. In that fine and instructive old book,
M. Blundeville His Exercises, printed at London in 1594, the second
chapter of "the second part of the Spheare " treats "of the Fire and
of his nature and motion " as follows : "The fire is an element most
hoat and dry, pure, subtill, and so clear as it doth not hinder our
sight looking through the same towards the stars, and is placed next
to the Spheare of the Moon, under the which it is turned about like
a celestial Spheare."

Page 81.

"It tears
The firmament in eight-and-forty shares."

In the catalogue of Hipparchus, preserved in the Almagest of Ptol-
emy, the stars were divided into forty-eight constellations.

Page 82.

"And in these constellations then arise
New stars."

It was the apparition of a new star in 1572, in the constellation of
Cassiopeia, that turned Tycho Brahe to astronomy ; and a new bright
star in Ophiuchus, in 1604, had excited general wonder, and afforded
Galileo a text for an attack on the Ptolemaic system.

Page 82.

" Doth not a Tenarus or higher hill."

Donne here uses Tenarus for the great peak of Teneriffe, than which there can be hardly a higher-seeming hill, rising, as it does, almost from the shore, to a height of about 12,000 feet above the sea-level.

Page 83.

" Whom had that ancient seen, who thought souls made
Of harmony."

Probably Donne means by " that ancient " Simmias, who maintains this doctrine in Plato's *Phædo*.

Page 84.

. . . "if those great doctors truly said
That the ark to man's proportiön was made."

St. Augustine is, perhaps, the most famous of the great doctors who propounded this notion. See *De Civitate Dei*, xv, 26.

Page 86.

" What artist now dares boast that he can bring
Heaven hither, or constellate any thing . . ."

The meaning of "constellate" as here used is explained by the next three verses.

Page 88.

. . . " if I
Were punctual in this Anatomy."

" If I were punctual "— if I treated of my subject point by point.

Page 91.

" What is 't to us, alas ! if there have been
An Angel made a Throne or Cherubin ? "

What is it to us if an angel be raised to one of the higher orders of the Heavenly Hierarchy ?

Page 92.

" Fate did but usher her
To years of reason's use, and then infer
Her destiny to herself."

This use of "infer" in the sense of "commit," or "intrust," is unusual.

Page 93.

Of the Progress of the Soul. The Harbinger.

"Thy glorious journals in that blessed state ? "

"Journals "—course of existence.

Page 97.

The Second Anniversary.

" For though to err be worst, to try truths forth .

"Forth "—thoroughly, to the end, as in the verse:
"Whom it concerns to hear this matter forth."
Measure for Measure, v, 1, 255.

Page 97.

"Because she was the form that made it live."

"Form" used here in its scholastic sense for that which gives its individuality to any natural object. "Omnis forma corporalis est forma indivuata per materiam, et determinata ad hic et nunc." St. Th. Aquinas, *Summa Theol.*, I, cx, 1. "Illud quo primo aliquid operatur est forma ejus." *Id.*, I, lxxvi, 1.

Page 98.

"And think those broken and soft notes to be
Division."

"Division," a series of notes forming one melodic sequence, as in ditties
"Sung by a fair queen in a summer's bower,
With ravishing division, to her lute."
1 *Henry IV.*, iii, 1, 211.

Page 99.

"Lays thee to sleep but a Saint Lucy's night."
The longest night of the year, December 13, old style.

Page 99.

"That which of her ingredients should invade
  The other three."
According to the schoolmen the body was composed of the four elements.

Page 100.

"Think but how poor thou wast, how óbnoxious."
"Obnoxious"—exposed to harm; as Milton says:

> "Obnoxious first or last
To basest things." P. L., ix, 170.

Page 103.

"She, of whose soul if we may say 't was gold,
  Her body was th' electrum, and did hold
  Many degrees of that."
Electrum was composed of four parts gold and one part silver. Pliny, Nat. Hist., xxxiii, 23.

Page 106.

"Are there not some Courts (and then no things be
  So like as Courts)."
All courts, then, let us see that libelers do not exaggerate the ill to be found in them, because they — the courts — do more ill than the libelers can declare.

Page 106.

"Where thou shalt see the blessed Mother-maid
  Joy in not being that which men have said."
Joy in not being "sine labe concepta," for then she would have had no virtue in being good.

Page 107.

"She who hath carried thither new degrees
(As to their number) to their dignities."

She who, by being added to the saints, has increased the number of their orders.

Page 109.

"Be sought alone, and not in such a thrust."

"Thrust"—crowd.

Page 113.

Elegy on Prince Henry.

The death of Prince Henry, eldest son of James I., on November 6, 1612, gave occasion to innumerable productions in verse by the court poets and others, full, for the most part, of servile adulation. Bacon wrote a brief "character" of him, which may serve to illustrate Donne's poem. See Spedding's *Bacon*, vi, 323.

Drummond reports Jonson as saying "that Donne said to him he wrote that Epitaph on Prince Henry, *Look to me, Faith*, to match Sir Ed. Herbert in obscureness." *Conversations*, p. 8.

Page 113.

"Quotidian things and equidistant hence."

All natural things as objects of reason may be regarded as equally distant.

Page 114.

"For whom what princes angled, when they tried."

"What princes angled"—those princes who angled. "And others studies" (two lines lower) should read, I believe, "And others studied."

Page 116.

"Oh may I (since I live) but see or hear
That she-intelligence which moved this sphere."

The allusion in these and the subsequent verses is inexplicable.

Page 117.

Obsequies to the Lord Harrington.

John, Lord Harington, was the only and much younger brother of the Countess of Bedford. He was not yet twenty-two years old when he died, February 27, 1613. He had lately returned from the Continent, where he had been traveling with a tutor. His tutor had died, and he came home ill, and the report was spread that they had been poisoned by the Jesuits. He seems to have possessed such qualities and to have given such promise that his early death was a true grief to his family, and a cause of genuine regret to all who knew him. A sketch of his character, in the main derived from a funeral sermon by Richard Stocks, pastor of Allhallows, London, is to be found in H. Harington's *Nugæ Antiquæ*, London, 1804, ii, 307. Fuller says of him : ''He did not count himself privileged from being good, by being great ; and his timely piety, rising early, did not soon after go to bed, . . . but continued watchful during his life." *Worthies*, edited by Nuttall, iii, 290.

Page 117.

"But, Madam, since your noble brother's fortune being yours."

Lord Harington bequeathed two thirds of his fortune to the Countess of Bedford, and one third to his other sister, Anne, wife of Sir Robert Chichester.

Page 119.

"Yet are the trunks which do to us derive
Things in proportion."

"Trunk"—Milton's "glazed optic tube," a telescope.

Page 121.

"Yea, and those small ones which the poles engrave."
"Engrave"—encircle.

Page 126.

"As Saxon wives and French soldarii did."

"Soldarii" is a mistaken reading for *soldurii*, the *devoti* of whom Cæsar speaks (*De Bello Gall.*, iii. 22), who died with their friends.

Page 126.

" Grief in great Alexander's great excess "—
On Hephaestion's death. See Plutarch's *Life of Alexander*, c. 72.

Page 127.

An Elegy on the Lady Markham.

Bridget, Lady Markham, was the daughter of Sir James Harington, Bart., and cousin to the Countess of Bedford. She died on
March 4, 1609. See *ante*, note on p. 62.

Page 127.

"As men of China, after an age's stay,
 Do take up porcelain where they buried clay."

In Ramusio's version of Marco Polo the manner of making porcelain is thus described: "They excavate a certain kind of earth, as it
were from a mine, and this they heap into great piles, and then leave
it undisturbed and exposed to wind, rain, and sun for thirty or forty
years. In this space of time the earth becomes sufficiently refined for
the manufacture of porcelain." "The story," says Colonel Yule, "of
the life-long period during which the porcelain clay was exposed to
temper long held its ground." (Yule's *Book of Sir Marco Polo*, ii,
225.) Bacon, in his *Historia Densi et Rari*, narrates the story, giving
credence to it.

Pages 127, 128.

"So at this grave, her limbec . . .
          . . . her soul shall inspire."

The phraseology of this passage is alchemical, and the meaning
seems to be : Her soul shall be the alembic in which her flesh shall be
distilled into such stuff that it shall serve as the tincture or elixir
to transmute everything into similar precious material.

Page 128.

"They perish both, when they attempt the just."

Both deaths perish when the just die, for carnal death has no
power over our soul, and spiritual death has no power over the good.

Page 128.

"So, unobnoxious now, she hath buried both."

"Unobnoxious"—not subject to hurt.

Page 128.

"How little poison cracks a crystal glass!"

"And though it be said that poison will break a Venice glass, yet have we not met any of that nature." Sir Thomas Browne, *Vulgar and Common Errors*, vii, ch. 17.

Page 129.

Elegy on Mistress Boulstred.

Of Mistress Boulstred little seems to be known. Jonson's coarse Epigram, No. LXVII, *On the Court Pucelle*, was written on her. He told Drummond that it "was stolen out of his pocket by a gentleman who drank him drowsy, and given Mistress Boulstraid, which brought him great displeasure." (*Conversations*, p. 38.) She was a friend of the Countess of Bedford, and died at her house in August, 1609. Donne gives a report of her fatal illness in a letter to Sir Henry Goodyere. *Letters*, p. 215.

Page 129.

"Death, I recant, and say unsaid by me."

This verse would be better printed,

"Death I recant and say, Unsaid by me," etc.

Page 129.

"Into his bloody, or plaguy, or starved jaws."

"Plaguy"—used here, as elsewhere, by Donne, as an adjective formed from the substantive "plague."

Page 135.

Elegy on the Lord Chancellor.

Thomas Egerton, Lord Ellesmere, and finally Lord Brackley, died in the spring of 1617. He deserved Donne's eulogy. He was by all accounts a grave, wise, high-minded man. Donne had known him well, for as a young man he had been his secretary for five years, and it was while in this employment that he fell in love with, and clandestinely married, the young niece of Lady Ellesmere. The marriage caused his dismissal from the Lord Chancellor's service.

Page 136.

Elegy.

Dr. Grosart prints this from a manuscript as, " Upon the death of Mrs. Boulstred."

Page 137.

" We had had a saint, have now a holiday "—

That is, she would have been canonized at her death, and we should have now a holiday consecrated to her.

Page 138.

" Earth too, will be a Lemnia, and the tree
    That wraps that crystal in a wooden tomb,
    Shall be took up spruce filled with diamond."

A red clay found in the island of Lemnos and known as *terra Lemnia* had repute in antiquity as an antidote to poison. (See Pliny, *N. H.*, xxv, 13.) It was used in the middle ages as one of very many ingredients of the *theriaca*, and is said to be still employed as a drug in Turkey. By some of the alchemists the name was given to the essential component of the Philosopher's Stone. "Corpus igitur nostrum, quod vulgo dicitur Terra Lemnia," says "Philalethes" in the *Fons Chemicæ Philosophiæ* (Musæum Hermeticum, Frankfort, 1678, p. 800). It is in this sense, I believe, that Donne here uses the word "Lemnia." The earth will be a Lemnia — that is, will transmute the crystal into pure diamond.

Page 138.

An Hymn to the Saints, and to Marquess Hamilton.

The Sir Robert Carr, or Kerr, to whom the letter preceding this poem is addressed was one of the Scotch favorites of King James and of Prince Charles. In 1633 he was created Earl of Ancrum. He was always about the court, and was one of the courtiers to whom Donne had looked for preferment, and whose "very humble and thankful servant in Christ Jesus" he professed himself to be. Several of Donne's printed letters are addressed to him; their tone is of mingled friendliness and servility. He was second cousin of James's special favorite, Carr, Earl of Somerset.

James, second Marquis of Hamilton, born 1589, died 1624, was one of the chief favorites and intimates of King James. The man who occupied this position is not likely to have been a saint. He was possessed of good looks and a lively disposition, and these characteristics are referred to in Donne's curious Elegy. See Clarendon's character of him, *History of the Rebellion*, 1819, i, 230.

Page 138.

"And even then I did best, when I had least truth for my subjects."

The reference is perhaps to the poems on Mrs. Elizabeth Drury.

Page 140.

"Never made body such haste to confess
What a soul was."

This alludes to what Wilson tells of in his *Life and Reign of King James the First.* "The Marquis Hamilton died before our King, suspected to be poisoned, the symptoms being very presumptuous; his head and body swelling to an excessive greatness; the body being all over full of great blisters, with variety of colours. The hair of his head and beard came off without being touched, and brought the skin with them; and there was great clamour of it in the court, so that doctors were sent for to view the body; but the matter was huddled up, and little spoken of." Wilson, in Kennett's *History of England*, ii, 789.

The suspicion of poison as the cause of death of eminent persons was frequent in James's reign. In Overbury's case there is little doubt of the poisoning ; but the rumor of it, with or without foundation, was spread concerning the death of Prince Henry, of Lord Harington, of the Queen and of the King, and of others.

The close of the Elegy is instructive as regards the difficulty of transforming the marquis into a saint, and both the letter to Sir Robert Carr and the Elegy itself afford remarkable illustration of Donne's nature in his latter years. It is not easy to reconcile genuine piety and reverence for divine things with such adulatory insincerities. The four verses beginning ''And who shall dare to ask them'' are of his best.

Page 159.

The Cross.

> ''As perchance carvers do not faces make,
> But that away, which hid them there, do take.''

This couplet bears some likeness to the famous verses of Michelangelo,

> ''Non ha l'ottimo artista alcun concetto
> Ch'un marmo solo in se non circonscriva
> Col suo soverchio, e solo a quello arriva
> La man che obbedisce all' intelletto.''

Page 160.

Resurrection.

> ''He was all gold when he lay down, but rose
> All tincture.''

In the mystical jargon of the alchemists ''tincture'' was the designation of the spiritual principle by which the product of their art was capable of transmuting and transubstantiating other substances into likeness to its own. Its meaning is darkly set forth in the *Liber Alze de Lapide Philosophico*, which may be found in the *Musæum Hermeticum*, Frankfort, 1676, p. 323. In an anonymous rhymed alchemical treatise printed by Elias Ashmole in his curious *Theatrum Chemicum Britannicum*, London, 1652, the writer says, page 409,

> ''Then tincture of gold is a most noble thing,''

and it is to this tincture that Donne refers.

II.—18

Page 161.

The Annunciation and Passion.

Dr. Grosart, in his edition of Donne's *Poems*, 1873, gives the full title of this poem, from a manuscript, as : "Upon the Annunciation and Passion falling upon one day, 1608."

Page 162.

"Or as creation he hath made, as God,
    With the last judgment but one period."

"Of God himself, it is safely resolved in the School, that he never did any thing in any part of time of which he had not an eternal preconception." Donne, *Sermons*, 1640, Sermon LXVI, p. 667. E.

Page 163.

Good Friday, 1613.

"The intelligence that moves, devotion is."

Intelligence is here used as by the schoolmen, by whom the angels who imparted motion to the heavenly spheres were named "intelligences."

Page 163.

"But that Christ on this cross did rise and fall."

It should have been noted in a foot-note to the text that all editions after that of 1633 give this verse, correctly,

"But that Christ on his cross did rise and fall."

Page 164.

The Litany.

In a letter to Sir H. Goodyere, which seems to have been written in 1610, Donne writes from his bed, to which he was confined by illness : "Since my imprisonment in my bed, I have made a meditation in verse, which I called a Litany ; the word you know imports no other than supplication . . . and though a copy of it were due to you now, yet I am so unable to serve myself with writing it for you at this time, being some thirty staves of nine lines, that I must intreat you to take a promise that you shall have the first, as a testimony to that duty which I owe to your love, and to myself who am bound to cherish it by my best offices. That by which it will deserve best acceptation is, that neither the Roman church need call it defective, because it abhors not the particular mention of the blessed Triumphers in heaven ; nor the Reformed can deservedly accuse it of attributing more than a rectified devotion ought to do."

In a later portion of the letter there is a break, occasioned by the omission of some words, after which comes the following curious and interesting passage : "— opinion of the song, not that I make such trifles for praise, but because as long as you speak comparatively of it with mine own and not absolutely, so long I am of your opinion ; even at this time, when (I humbly thank God) I ask and have his comfort of sadder meditations, I do not condemn in myself that I have given my wit such evaporations as those, if they be free from profaneness, or obscene provocations." *Letters*, pp. 32, 36.

Donne's "better angel" and his "worser spirit" seem to have kept up a continual contest, now the one, now the other, gaining the mastery in his

"Poor soul, the centre of his sinful earth."

Page 168.

Stanza X.

"Thou in thy scattered mystic body would'st
In Abel die."

By the medieval church Abel was regarded as a type of Christ, not only as righteous in the sight of God, but also as the first martyr. Jeremy Taylor in his *Life and Death of Jesus*, describing the crucifixion, says : "But now Abel is led forth by his brother to be slain." *Works*, 1822, III, 372.

Page 170.

Stanza XIV.

"Since to be graciöus
Our task is treble."

"Gracious"— acceptable ; or, perhaps, recipients of grace.

Page 174.

Stanza XXVI.

The last three verses of this stanza are obscure. The meaning seems to be : When these men wrongfully accuse us, and, in doing so, decline from thee, may they see us, notwithstanding, listen to them to our own amendment, and do thou, Lord, lock thine ears to the injustice.

Page 176.

Upon the Translation of the Psalms by Sir Philip Sydney and the Countess of Pembroke his Sister.

This translation was not printed complete till 1822. The version of the one hundred and thirty-seventh Psalm was published in 1713, in the *Guardian*, No. 18.

Page 181.

To Mr. Tilman.

> " Mary's prerogative was to bear Christ ; so
>   'T is preachers' to convey him ; for they do,
>   As angels out of clouds, from pulpits speak."

"A preacher in earnest," says Walton of Donne, " weeping some-times for his auditory, sometimes with them, always preaching to himself, like an angel from a cloud, though in none."

Page 181.

> "If then th' astronomers, whereas they spy
>   A new-found star, their optics magnify"—

That is, celebrate, magnify the worth of the glasses with which they have spied the new star.

Page 181.

A Hymn to Christ, at the Author's last going into Germany.

Donne's last going to Germany was with Lord Doncaster in 1619. See *ante*, note on p. 41.

Page 183.

The Lamentations of Jeremy. For the most part according to Tremelius.

Tremellius (born 1510 ?, died 1580) was an Italian Hebraist of some distinction. He was for a time in England. He published a Latin translation of the Bible which ran through many editions, but fell into disrepute because of its lack of fidelity to the original.

Page 200.

Hymn to God, my God, in my Sickness.

"We think that Paradise and Calvary,
Christ's cross and Adam's tree, stood in one place."

As already stated (see note on Vol. I, p. 194), I know not the source of this fancy.

Page 203.

Translation.

In previous editions the first two verses of this poem have been printed as its title.

Page 205.

De Libro, etc.

The third and fourth verses seem inserted out of place; standing as they do, they admit of no easy explanation.

ELEGIES UPON THE AUTHOR.

Page 209.

To the Memory of my ever desired friend Doctor Donne.

Henry King (born 1591, died 1669), the author of this Elegy, was successively canon of Christ Church, dean of Rochester, and, 1641, bishop of Chichester. "A most florid preacher," says Anthony à Wood. "When he was young he delighted much in studies of music and poetry." In a letter written in 1664, and prefixed to the first edition of Walton's *Life of Hooker*, Dr. King speaks of his

II.—18*

"most dear and incomparable friend Dr. Donne, late Dean of St.
Paul's Church, who not only trusted me as his Executor, but three
days before his death delivered into my hands those excellent Sermons of his now made public, professing before Dr. Winniff, Dr.
Montfort, and, I think, yourself, then present at his bedside, that it
was by my restless importunity that he had prepared them for the
Press.   Together with which (as his best Legacy) he gave me all his
Sermon-Notes and his other Papers containing an Extract of near
Fifteen hundred Authors.   How these were got out of my hands, you
who were the Messenger for them, and how lost both to me and
yourself, is not now seasonable to complain : but, since they did mis-
carry, I am glad that the general Demonstration of his Worth was
so fairly preserv'd, and represented to the World by your Pen in the
History of his Life ; indeed so well that beside others, the best Critic
of our later time, (Mr. John Hales of Eaton College) affirm'd to me,
He had not seen a life written with more advantage to the Subject or
more reputation to the Writer than that of Dr. Donnes."

By his will Donne left to Dr. King, according to Walton's state-
ment, "that medal of gold of the Synod of Dort with which the
States presented him at his last being at the Hague, and the two
pictures of Padre Paolo and Fulgentio, men of his acquaintance when
he travelled Italy, and of great note in that nation for their remarkable learning."

Walton tells us that, just before his death, Donne, having resolved
to have a monument made, "sent for a carver to make for him in
wood the figure of an urn, giving him directions for the compass and
height of it, and to bring with it a board of the just height of his
body. 'These being got, then without delay a choice painter was got
to be in readiness to draw his picture, which was taken as followeth :
Several charcoal fires being first made in his large study he brought
with him into that place his winding-sheet in his hand, and, having
put off all his clothes, had this sheet put on him, and so tied with
knots at his head and feet, and his hands so placed as dead bodies
are usually fitted, to be shrouded and put into their coffin or grave.
Upon this urn he then stood, with his eyes shut, and with so much of

the sheet turned aside as might show his lean, pale and deathlike face, which was purposely turned toward the East, from whence he expected the second coming of his and our Saviour Jesus.' In this posture he was drawn at his just height, and when the picture was fully finished he caused it to be set by his bedside, where it continued and became his hourly object till his death, and was then given to his dearest friend and executor, Dr. Henry King, then chief Residentiary of St. Paul's, who caused him to be carved in one entire piece of white marble, as it now stands in that church."

Page 210.

"Thou, like the dying swan, didst lately sing
Thy mournful dirge in audience of the King."

Walton, in his *Life of Donne*, gives a striking account of Donne's appearance on this occasion. His text was: "To God the Lord belong the issues from death." "Many that then saw his tears and heard his faint and hollow voice, professed they thought the text prophetically chosen, and that Dr. Donne had preached his own funeral sermon."

Page 215.

On the Death of Doctor Donne.

The author of this Elegy, Edward Hyde, D. D., was, at the date of Donne's death, fellow of Christ Church, afterward rector of Brightwell, near Wallingford, in Berkshire ; he was noted, in later years, as a royalist preacher and author of several now forgotten theological treatises.

Page 216.

On Doctor Donne, by Dr. C. B. of O.

Richard Corbet, born 1582, died 1635 ; bishop of Oxford 1629, of Norwich 1632. In his youth, says Anthony à Wood, he was "esteemed one of the most celebrated wits in the University [Oxford], as his poems, jests, romantic fancies and exploits which he made and performed extemporary show. Afterwards entering into holy orders he became a most quaint preacher, and therefore much followed by ingenious men." Fuller speaks of him "as a high wit and most excellent poet." He was fond of a jest, and many of his poems are in a light vein. They have been frequently printed.

Page 219.

An Elegy upon Doctor Donne.

"Walton's first appearance as an author was in an elegy, which, after the fashion of the day, accompanied the first edition of Donne's poems. This species of verse, whether in the writing or the reading, is generally the most dreary compulsory labor to which man can be doomed. . . . I should be yielding to my partiality for Walton if I called these verses poetry ; but there is at least, in the eloquence of their honest sorrow, a tendency to become so which stops little short of it, and which is too often missed in the carefully cadenced ululation of similar efforts. Here, indeed, there seems no effort at all, and that surely is a crowning mercy. There is one phrase whose laconic pathos I find it hard to match elsewhere. It is where he bids his thought 'forget he loved me.' This is the true good-breeding of sorrow." Lowell, *Walton. Latest Literary Essays*, p. 69.

One other phrase is worth noting for the justness of its epithet, where Walton speaks of his own "mild pen."

Page 222.

Elegy on D. D.

These strained verses do little justice to the abilities of the ill-fated Sidney Godolphin (born 1610, died 1643), as they are reported by Clarendon and by Hobbes. "There was never," says the former in his *Life*, "so great a mind and spirit contained in so little room ; so large an understanding, and so unrestrained a fancy, in so very small a body," p. 24. And again, in his *History of the Rebellion*, telling of Godolphin's lamentable death, Clarendon speaks of him as "a young gentleman of incomparable parts." Hobbes, seldom in accord with Clarendon, says : "I have known clearness of judgment, and largeness of fancy ; strength of reason and graceful elocution ; a courage for the war and a fear for the laws, and all eminently in one man ; and that was my most noble and honoured friend Mr. Sidney Godolphin." *Leviathan*, 1651, p. 390.

It may be noted in excuse for the lack of merit in this Elegy that Godolphin was not much more than twenty-one years old when it was written. It is not wholly devoid of evidence of sincerity.

Page 224.

On Dr. John Donne.

Walton, in his *Life of Donne*, cites some verses of this Elegy, introducing them as follows : "There may be some that may incline to think . . . that my affection to my friend hath transported me to an immoderate commendation of his preaching. If this meets with any such, let me entreat . . . that they will receive a double witness for what I say ; it being attested by a gentleman of worth, Mr. Chidley, a frequent hearer of his sermons, in part of a funeral elegy writ by him on Mr. Donne ; and is a known truth though it be in verse."

Page 227.

An Elegy upon the Death of the Dean of Paul's. By Mr. Tho: Cary.

The name of the author of this Elegy is given as Carie or Cary in all the early editions, by mistake for Carew, in whose works it appears with some slight variations in its text.

Page 231.

An Elegy on Dr. Donne.

Sir Lucius Cary, better known as Lord Falkland, was but twenty years old when he wrote this Elegy. Full as it is of the defects common to much of the verse of the time,—of tasteless conceits and exaggerated sentiment,—it yet contains some lines which both illustrate and confirm Lord Clarendon's well-known splendid eulogy of him, one of the finest of the "characters" which give distinction to Clarendon's History.

Page 234.

On Dr. Donne's Death: by Mr. Mayne.

Jasper Mayne (born 1604, died 1672) in his earlier years wrote many plays and poems. He entered the church and became arch-deacon of Chichester.

Page 237.

Upon Mr. J. Donne and his Poems.

Arthur Wilson, who wrote these verses, in which there is more of the spirit of poetry than in most of the other elegies on Donne, was born in 1595 and died in 1652. He was well bred; he was secretary and groom of the chambers to Robert, Earl of Essex, and afterward steward of Robert, Earl of Warwick; he wrote some plays and poems, but is best known by his *Life and Reign of King James the First*, 1653, a curious and entertaining book.

Page 243.

Epitaph upon Dr. Donne.

Endymion Porter, the author of this Epitaph, was one of the courtiers with whom Donne must have been long familiar. Anthony à Wood speaks of him as "that great patron of all ingenious men, especially of poets; . . . a great man and beloved by two kings, James I. for his admirable wit, and Charles I. (to whom, as to his father, he was a servant) for his general learning, brave skill, sweet temper, great experience, travels and modern languages." (*Athen. Oxon.*, iii, 2.) He was a favorite and dependent of Buckingham, whose niece he married, and he was reported to have made money by selling his master's favors; he was often employed on secret service, and, having seen much of the world, was altogether one of the best-known and best-equipped courtiers of a profligate and extravagant court. Several of Howell's Letters are addressed to him.

NOTE ON A MANUSCRIPT OF DONNE'S POEMS.

SINCE these volumes were printed, I have obtained from Mr. Quaritch a manuscript of Donne's Poems. In whose possession it had previously been, Mr. Quaritch is unable to inform me. It is undated, but it appears to have been written before the publication of the first edition of the poems in 1633. As is well known, manuscript collections of verses were often made in the early seventeenth century, but they, perhaps, more frequently consist of the poems of various authors than, like this, of a single poet. This manuscript forms a folio volume of 270 pages. It is in its original binding. The pages were slightly trimmed by the binder, so that in a few cases a part of a word in the margin has been cut off. The writing is uniform, and easily legible. The scribe was somewhat careless, and did not revise his work, for it exhibits many obvious errors and oversights. In a few instances omissions of words occur, of such sort as to indicate that the text which the copyist had before him was either imperfect or illegible. But, as a whole, the copy is not deficient in completeness or correctness. The volume has no title. Whether it originally had one or not is uncertain, for one leaf (possibly two, corresponding to two blank leaves at the end) has been torn out at the beginning. It begins with four of the Satires, after which follow the other poems in no regular order, and in no groups except that most of the Letters are consecutive, and the Divine Poems are placed together near the end.

The manuscript contains all the poems printed in these volumes with the following exceptions : Vol. I, "Love's Usury," p. 11; "Lovers' Infiniteness," p. 16 ; "Song," p. 71 ; "Farewell to Love," p. 72 ; "The Token," p. 75 ; "Elegies" XII to XV, pp. 101–109 ; "Elegy," p. 122 ; "Upon Coryat's Crudities," p. 125 ; "Satire VI," p. 170 ; and five of the "Epigrams," pp. 184–186. Vol. II, "To the E. of D.," p. 41 ; "To the Countess of Huntingdon, p. 48 ; "A Dialogue," p. 53 ; "To the Countess of Bedford," p. 55 ; "To Ben Jonson," p. 66 ; "To Sir Thomas Roe," p. 67 ; "An Anatomy of the World," p. 71 ; "On the Progress of the Soul," p. 93 ; "Elegy on Mrs. Boulstred," p. 132; "On Himself," p. 133; "Elegy on the Lord C.," p. 135; "An Hymn to the Saints, and to Marquess Hamilton," p. 138; "On the Blessed Virgin Mary," p. 157; "Upon the Translation of the Psalms by Sir Philip Sidney and his Sister," p. 176; "Ode," p. 178; "To Mr. Tilman," p. 179; "Hymn to God, my God, in my Sickness," p. 199; "To Mr. George Herbert," p. 202; "Amicissimo et meritissimo Ben. Jonson," p. 204; "De Libro," etc., p. 205.

The most important omission, that of the two poems on Mrs. Elizabeth Drury ("An Anatomy of the World" and the "Progress of the Soul"), is to be accounted for by the fact that they had already been printed, and were thus obtainable. It is further to be noted that all but six of the other omitted pieces are not found in the first edition of the Poems, that of 1633, thus indicating that they were gathered up from scattered sources after its publication.

The volume contains a few poems not by Donne, and its last pages (pp. 243-270) are occupied by Donne's "Paradoxes," which were first printed in 1652.

The manuscript affords many various readings, most of them mere differences of "the" and "this," "these" and "those," and the like, but a few which afford a genuine correction, or a different reading of some interest. I append here a list of the more important of them, italicizing the changed words and marks of punctuation.

C. E. N.

October, 1895.

VARIOUS READINGS.

VOLUME I.

p. 6, l. 12.   And last till you *writ* your letter,
p. 12, last line. When did my *cold* a forward spring remove?
p. 19, l. 2.   That myself *(that 's you, not I)*
p. 19, l. 15.   I *thought* to send that heart instead of mine,
p. 22, last lines. And that I *love* my heart, and *love it* so
               That I would not from him that *hath it* go.
p. 30, l. 7.   Vandals and Goths *inundate* us,
p. 30, l. 21.   And how prerogative *those rights* devours,
p. 31, l. 3.   *Law* and their art alike it deadly wounds,

NOTE ON A MANUSCRIPT.

p. 36, l. 2.   One *should* but one man know;

p. 37, l. 19.   That love is weak where fear *is* strong as he;

p. 47, l. 5.   What I *shall* say I will not tell thee now,

p. 48, l. 10.   Mine would have taught *thy* heart to show

p. 54, l. 17.   Love *might* make me leave loving, or might try

p. 63, l. 17.   I would that age *were* by this paper taught

p. 75, l. 5.   And his *first* minute after noon is night.

p. 84, l. 1, 2.   Likeness glues love ; *then if so thou do,*
                  To make us *alike* and love must I change too ?

p. 88, l. 5.   Did *nourish* it, who now 's grown strong enough

p. 93, l. 11.   And *such* in searching wounds the surgeon is,

p. 94, l. 11.   And here, till *her,* which must be his death, come,

p. 99, l. 1.   I would not spit to quench the fire they *were* in,

p. 99, l. 20.   He say 't will ne'er be found, *oh !* be content;

p. 115, l. 19.   As *beauty is not* nor wealth; he that strays thus

p. 116, l. 11.   The nose (like to the *first* meridian) runs

p. 116, l. 24.   O'er passed, *and the straight* Hellespont, between

p. 117, l. 2.   Yet ere thou be where thou *wouldst* be embayed,

p. 117, l. 24.   Than if at beauty's *elements* he stay.

p. 118, l. 13,14. Your *gown's* going-off such beauteous state reveals,
                  As when *from* flowery meads th' hill's shadow steals.

p. 120, l. 4.   Which my *love's* masculine persuasive force

p. 138, l. 15.   In the *East India* fleet, because thou hast

p. 138, l. 19.   The earth doth in her *inward* bowels hold

p. 157, l. 23.   One would move love by *rhymes,* but witchcraft's
                  charms

p. 159, l. 19.   Law practice for mere gain, *hold* soul-repute

p. 159, l. 26.   Like a king's favorite, *yea,* like a king;

p. 170, l.10–12. One of our giant statutes ope his jaw
                  To suck me in ; for, hearing him, I found
                  That as burnt venom*ed* lechers do grow sound

p. 177, l. 12.   Of men, so in law, nails are *th'* extremities;

p. 190, l. 8.   For I *would* have no such readers

p. 190, l. 13.   *musheron*

p. 202, l. 9.   Pace with *his* native stream this fish doth keep,

VOLUME II.

p. 9,   l. 16.   In cities, blocks, and in lewd *courts*, devils.

p. 11, last line.   With women's milk and pap unto *her* end.

p. 15,   l. 9.   But that the next to him *is still* worse than he.

p. 37,   l. 19.   My *Muse* (for I had one) because I 'm cold

p. 39,   l. 5.   Perchance *this* Spanish business being done,

p. 39,   l. 7.   *Eclipsed* the light which Guiana would give,

p. 40.   Heading of poem.   To Mr. I. *L.*

p. 43,   l. 4.   Than I have done your *noble* wanting-it.

p. 47,   l. 1.   Care not then, Madam, how low your *praisers* lie;

p. 47,   l. 15.   May in your through-shine front *your* heart's thoughts see.

p. 47,   l. 19.   Of such were temples ; so and *of* such you are;

p. 60,   l. 9.   *When* he that would be good is thought by all

p. 63,   l. 12.   Her flesh rests in the earth as in *a* bed,

p. 123,   l. 13.   Which *now* I would not name, but that I see

p. 126, l. 7.   Prerogative hath thus dispensed *for* thee

p. 136.   Heading of poem.   Elegy *upon the death of Mrs. Boulstred.*

p. 143,   l. 11.   *This* first last end, now zealously possest

p. 145,   l. 11.   But as, for one which hath long *tasks*, 't is good

p. 145,   l. 20.   Alas! and do, unto *him* th' immaculate,

p. 146,   l. 10.   Death whom thy death slew ; nor shall *now* to me

p. 146, l. 16.   May then sin's sleep, and *death's* soon from me pass,

p. 155,   l. 4.   This beauteous form *assures* a piteous mind.

p. 160, l. 1.   Then doth the Cross of Christ work *fruitfully*

p. 162, l. 15.   This Church, by letting *these* days join, hath shown

p. 163, l. 13.   But that Christ on *his* cross did rise and fall,

p. 169, l. 9.   And call chaste *widowhood* virginity.

p. 186, l. 13.   Of all which *hear me* mourn, none comforts me;

p. 193, l. 18.   They have shut my life and cast *on me* a stone.

p. 201, l. 2.   Which *is* my sin though it were done before ?

p. 201, l.15–18. But swear by thyself that at my death thy *Sun*
                 Shall shine as *it* shines now and heretofore;
                 And having done that, thou hast done,
                 I *have* no more.

www.ingramcontent.com/pod-product-compliance
Lightning Source LLC
Chambersburg PA
CBHW020506270326
41926CB00008B/759